"Lisa Monique Martin's book *Chasing Fire* allows the reader a private glimpse into the author's personal journey of faith. Laden with practical application and a treasure trove of inspiring testimonies, this work is both a laymen's instructional manual as well as an evangelistic primer. Kudos to this woman of integrity!"

Jimi Merrell, Pastor of Prayer and Outreach
Valley Christian Center, Dublin, CA

"The Psalmist once wrote that the thoughts of the Spirit toward us are so many that they outnumber the sand. Lisa, in *Chasing Fire* shows us in a personal and spiritual way how God communicates His love. Her journey will resonate with you and sharpen your mind that God desires to speak to you in a variety of ways no matter what season is occurring on the path you are on."

Jonathan West, Associate Pastor
Christian Center of Shreveport; Shreveport, LA

"*Chasing Fire* drew me in and kept me longing for more. I was captivated, not only by Lisa's moving testimonies and practical insights of hearing from God, but by the promise of healing and life-giving conversations with a living, breathing, speaking Savior who is waiting to commune intimately with me. The challenge to take God at His word and wait expectantly and patiently to hear His voice has rocked my soul and motivated me to dig deeper and listen longer. The very practical teachings on how to hear and discern God's voice and how to recognize the different ways He speaks make this a great resource for anyone endeavoring to better discover God's will. The real life testimonies of fellow God-listeners brought Lisa's teachings to life and encouraged me to believe God for more! I love this book and can't wait to share it with the women in my church!"

Mary Anne Kent, Director of Women's Ministry
Northwest Fellowship Church, Austin, Texas

"This is a book you will read more than once. Lisa faces the myths and misconceptions about talking with and hearing the voice of God head on and gives practical answers in personal testimonies from her own life experience.

"The Bible tells us that we live in two worlds, the spiritual and physical. Those who live in the spiritual do not always have supernatural experiences, yet Lisa is not surprised by them and has learned to expect them. Reading about her journey, along with the scriptural references that support her interactions with God, reveals how God has transformed and built her character. This life of wonder can be yours and mine if we are open to the possibility of the depth of relationship with God that Lisa writes about in this book."

Eugene Richardson
Humanitarian, Seeds of Hope, Israel/Westbank

"Lisa Monique Martin is a powerful example that God is actively involved in His children's lives. Her simple faith and life are evidence that God wants to speak to us in a variety of ways, and that He is always there to guide and encourage—if we will only take the time to listen.

"This book is for anyone who desires a more vibrant walk with God or feels they are experiencing more religion than relationship with Jesus. Lisa will personally inspire you with her stories of faith to live an adventure with the Savior."

Shana Schutte, author, speaker,
and radio host of "The Beyond Imagination Minute"

Chasing Fire

Lisa Monique Martin

E ergreen PRESS

Mobile, Alabama

Chasing Fire
by Lisa Monique Martin
Copyright ©2014 Lisa Monique Martin

All rights reserved. This book is protected under the copyright laws of the United States of America. This book may not be copied or reprinted for commercial gain or profit.

Scripture quotations marked NKJV are taken from the New King James Version®. Copyright © 1982 by Thomas Nelson, Inc. Used by permission. All rights reserved.

Scriptures marked NASB are taken from the *New American Standard Bible*, Copyright ©1960, 1962, 1963, 1968, 1971, 1973, 1975, 1977 by The Lockman Foundation.

Scriptures marked KJV are taken from the King James version of the Bible.

ISBN 978-1-58169-544-1
For Worldwide Distribution
Printed in the U.S.A.

Evergreen Press
P.O. Box 191540 • Mobile, AL 36619
800-367-8203

To the Three in One
who blessed me
with a life that is one
big encounter.
I love you so much.
Thank You, Abba!

Special Thanks

To my parents, Russell and Mary Ann Walker, who ensured the growth and development of my walk with Jesus, God given talents and spiritual gifts.

To my husband, Ron Martin, who lovingly sacrificed his time, energy, and resources to see this book come to pass.

To the following spiritual leaders whom God used to shape and push me into my callings and destiny: Stephen and Dr. Sally Beck, Jeff and Sandra Newman, Dr. J. Kie and Tina Bowman, John Paul and Diane Jackson, and John and Dawna Thomas.

Contents

1 There Is More 1

2 Your Name 12

3 His Presence 26

4 The Word 37

5 Correction From a Brotha' 48

6 A Sign To Encourage Us 59

7 Spirit Inspired 71

8 Supernatural Living 83

9 Seeing the Unseen 98

10 Dreams and Visions 110

11 Knowing the Unknown 124

12 Servants From Heaven 134

13 The God Zone 144

14 Recognizing and Listening 153

Acknowledgments

Thanks to the Walker and Douglas family for giving me strength for the journey and providing such a wonderful heritage that encourages me to carry the baton of legacy.

Thanks to the Stewart family for being a great role in the village I grew up in. You truly are family to me and I will continue to hold you in my heart and prayers.

Thanks to Cheryl Canfield, her brother, Bob Canfield, and the entire Canfield family who were an active part in getting me to where I am today. Thank all of you for your love and support. May God bring to you a hundred times the blessings you have graciously bestowed on me.

Thanks to my brothers and sisters in Christ who have maintained consistent and continual contact and encouragement over the past 10-35 years: Heidi Parres, Rick and Gina Prince, Jerry Bertrand, Sharon Scott, Amy Thomas, Eugene & Cecelia Richardson, Hal & Barbra Miner. I love you guys!

Thanks to my agent, Keith Carroll, who did not see an unknown writer, but one who is known by Christ. Thank you for believing in me and the call of Christ on my life, as well as, the message of this book. You are appreciated more than you know. God Bless You!

One

There Is More

I will never forget the night my team members and I were to be shot and killed.

We were warned that the military would be waiting to kill us on sight for breaking the law by holding revival meetings. In a small village in India, we had been sharing the gospel of Christ through acts of love, kindness, and the demonstration of the works of the Holy Spirit. People were healed, helped, and hugged. As God moved through the life circumstances and hearts of those with extreme need, their testimonies spread to neighboring villages.

For five days, we visited these villages with God under His power. His power was the invitation to learn about Him and eternal salvation at our revival meetings. By the time we had received the news regarding the military, there was no time to do anything but pray. After a short prayer and quick discussion, we followed the call to go. Their souls were worth it. We went despite the threat.

Chasing Fire

Many wonderful things took place on this short-term mission trip. God answered a longtime fervent prayer to come face to face with the miraculous. This particular night would prove to be His grand finale.

It was a hot and muggy night. I can still feel the ride on the bumpy road and taste the stale air. It would be the last night of the revival, the trip, and our lives. The war of fear vs. faith began. Faith helped our determination to praise our way into martyrdom. As we sang and clapped in time with the bumps in the road and squeaks of the van, fear crept into the shadows of my mind. What about my family? What about my pastor, church, and friends? Will they separate my team? What will they do with my body? Will I be raped first?

After the long drive to a field outside one of the small villages we had been serving in during the day, we found what we expected. Thousands of people had already gathered in prayer and worship. The small stage was set with one microphone, two speakers rigged to an old P.A. system, and worship leaders who led with only voices and tambourines. The night sky was our ceiling, flood lights our walls, and the military our exit doors.

As the van pulled in to park, I saw soldiers with rifles in hand, and my heart started to beat so hard, I swore I could hear it. The van came to a complete stop. When the engine stopped, everything went into slow motion. The singing, music, voices—all sounds echoed, muffled as if I were under water. These dull, elongated sounds became the musical score to the film of my life that ran across the screen of my mind.

Years of memory flooded in a few seconds. The driver had exited the van. I inhaled. He moved across the front of our vehicle and came around to its side to open the door. I exhaled. He reached the door leading to the Pearly Gates. *Inhale.* Death was eminent, eternity certain. I looked down. *Exhale.* I prayed a last prayer. "Jesus, receive Your maidservant. May my walk be pleasing to You. Please forgive my failings. I forgive all those who have harmed me. I love You, Jesus."

Inhale. The door opened. *Exhale.* The first team member exited.

Inhale. The second and third exited.

Exhale. Inhale. My turn. As I emerged from the van, the pace of life and all sounds returned to normal.

I walked to the front of the stage, fear lurking but strength entering me. I was at peace. Interestingly, the service continued. The word was preached, the blind were given sight, the crippled walked. People came to Christ, and praise and worship continued. The military was still there but seemed to be doing nothing but walking around.

"They're here for crowd control," I told a teammate. "Someone just tried to scare us off."

If only the story ended there. But it doesn't. It is much more glorious!

After many hours, the service concluded. We piled in the vans, made our way back to our hotel, and began our debriefing process with our leader. We shared testimonies of how the Lord moved and laughed at how we were deceived regarding the military. Then, just before our closing

Chasing Fire

prayer, a knock came at the door. It was hotel staff, asking our leader, John, to come to the lobby because two soldiers needed to talk to him.

We all looked at each other, frozen with silent surprise. John turned to us, his hand stretched out, palm down, as if to say, "It's okay. Don't worry." But his eyes and facial expression did not convey the same message.

He walked out, the door closed behind him, and we all let out a huge sigh or gasped because we'd been holding our breath. After a brief conversation filled with panic, we began to pray. We prayed and waited, prayed and waited.

After an hour, John burst in with smiles and laughter. "You guys are not going to believe what happened! I can't stay long. I have to go back, but those soldiers are freaking out!"

Catching his breath, he sat down and continued. "When I got downstairs, they dropped to my feet in tears, panicking and grabbing my pant legs. 'We need what you have,' they said, 'because if not, we will surely die!' Those soldiers had been sent here to kill us. They had orders to shoot on sight. But when we arrived, they couldn't do it. I asked them why, and they said, 'We could not touch you! We were powerless because of the giants surrounding you!'"

The soldiers feared for their lives because they did not follow a direct order. Interestingly, out of all the soldiers at the event, these two were the only ones who came to find out where the giants came from and how they could get the power demonstrated by the team.

That night, they came to Christ and were baptized immediately. The following morning we left for the next city.

This is one of many testimonies in my own experience with God. It is one of my favorite because the ending inspires awe, encouragement, deep thought, and even disbelief in those hearing it. Supernatural experiences don't surprise me. I expect them. After all, India was not the first time death came to my door—or the last. And every time, God's hand reached from His timeless heaven and saved me miraculously. My supernatural experiences with God are etched into the fiber of my being. He has used them to transform me, build my character, and renew my mind. My journey with the Creator through Christ has afforded me an abundant, adventurous life. This life of wonder would not be possible without the knowledge of the depth of God's love as I harness and use the resurrection power He gives when I listen to His voice.

From my childhood, the Lord has used my relationships with others to demonstrate that being a Christian is more than sitting in a pew and writing a check. These things are important, but with no spirit behind them, they become nothing more than a box to check on a to-do list. When our experiences line up with what we read in God's Word and we see what the pastor is preaching, serving and giving become just as natural as saying our names. God has more for us. God's heart is to be in our business by helping us to experience Him, His power, and His love. Wouldn't it be awesome to live in expectation of greatness and all that is good and seeing them happen throughout our lifetime?

This is what we have to consider. Do we want more than a mundane forty- to sixty-hour workweek that only pays the bills, or do we want to wake up every morning with the freshness of dew in our spirit and mind? Do we want confidence in calamity and steadfast clarity instead of confusion? Do we want to run instead of limp our way through life? Do we want to have peace whether prosperous or poor, knowing our circumstances are just a setup for the supernatural and miraculous to take place? Do we want an extraordinary life instead of an ordinary one? Do we want more?

Many of us have spent too much time living in fear, without hope, without clear direction, feeling powerless, and walking robotic-like through life. As a result we get nothing and nowhere in our spiritual life. This is a problem for those of us who want more. Something beckons the soul, creating a hunger that is not satisfied with a mundane, rote, and boring life. Happiness fades and emptiness occurs in the spirit and heart. We might share these feelings with others, and we may even whisper to ourselves, "There's got to be more than this."

There is. It begins with the One who spoke everything we see into existence and has the perfect life plan for every person born. God speaks. He needs you to hear Him if you're to embark on a life journey that will bring thrills, wonderment, joy, peace, satisfaction, and fulfillment. Everything in this book is biblically based, and the scripture itself brings validity to the experiences you will read about. These real-life experiences are to bring encouragement, spark inspiration, and whet appetites for supernatural living with a supernatural God.

Millions of people hear the Lord. Earthly title or rank

has nothing to do with His obsession to be in a one-on-one relationship with each of us. Who are we that He would want this? This is the same question King David posed in a psalm he penned.

When I look at your heavens, the work of your fingers, the moon and the stars, which you have set in place, what is man that you are mindful of him, and the son of man that you care for him? (Psalm 8:3-4, *The One New Man Bible*)

The answer:

But now, thus says the Lord, who created you, O Jacob, and He who formed you, O Israel: "Fear not, for I have redeemed you; I have called you by your name; You are Mine" (Isaiah 43:1, NKJV).

O Lord, You have searched me and known me. You know my sitting down and my rising up; You understand my thought afar off. You comprehend my path and my lying down, and are acquainted with all my ways. For there is not a word on my tongue, but behold, O Lord, You know it altogether. You have hedged me behind and before, and laid Your hand upon me. Such knowledge is too wonderful for me; it is high, I cannot attain it.

Where can I go from Your Spirit? Or where can I flee from Your presence? If I ascend into heaven, You are there; If I make my bed in hell, behold, You are there. If I take the wings of the morning, and dwell in the utter-

most parts of the sea, even there Your hand shall lead me, and Your right hand shall hold me. If I say, "Surely the darkness shall fall on me," even the night shall be light about me; indeed, the darkness shall not hide from You, but the night shines as the day; the darkness and the light are both alike to You.

For You formed my inward parts; You covered me in my mother's womb. I will praise You, for I am fearfully and wonderfully made; marvelous are Your works, and that my soul knows very well. My frame was not hidden from You, when I was made in secret, and skill-fully wrought in the lowest parts of the earth. Your eyes saw my substance, being yet unformed. And in Your book they all were written, the days fashioned for me, when as yet there were none of them. How precious also are Your thoughts to me, O God! How great is the sum of them! If I should count them, they would be more in number than the sand; when I awake, I am still with You. (Psalm 139:1-18, NKJV—a song written by King David and given to the chief musician for everyone to sing)

This song has come through thousands of years to reach us. Its purpose? To show us that God knows about each of us, He made each of us, He thinks about us, He is with us and has written our days in a book. The great God, the Creator of the universe, cares for all of us. He loves us. The love of God allows us through Christ to take part in the or-chestration of all He intends for the planet earth during our lifetime and beyond, into eternity. God wants to unleash us

There Is More

as beacons of hope—heroines and heroes in the lives of the suffering, brokenhearted, hopeless, poor in spirit, unhealthy, tormented, and bound.

God will use the tangible as well as the supernatural to accomplish this. Giving a thirsty person water or feeding the hungry is tangible and demonstrates God's love and care. The supernatural is God making it clear He is the author and finisher of life. He did this for my team by sending angelic protection and creating an invisible barrier that only the military could see. God produces miracles, signs, and wonders. These demonstrate God's deity, sovereignty, and power.

The words *miracle, signs*, and *wonder*, however, are often used improperly. Have you ever heard someone say that passing a test or getting out of a traffic ticket was a miracle? Those are not miracles; they are gifts of grace. I will admit that God's grace is a miracle because we don't deserve it. However, a miracle is an unexplainable happening. Jesus is a gift to the world, but His conception in a virgin is a miracle.

Miracles, signs, and wonders are events that can be explained only as supernatural acts of God. For example, the Bible tells us about people raised from the dead, physical healings by a word of prayer or command rather than earthly medical intervention, casting out demons by a verbal command, and people knowing or seeing the future.

We also read of an angel breaking men out of jail after they'd been imprisoned wrongfully or for the cause of Christ. And what about the small amount of food multiplied to feed thousands, or people hearing a foreign lan-

Chasing Fire

guage they didn't know and suddenly understanding what is being said? All these things are in the Bible. And all these things have taken place through regular people like you and me, in modern times, like the night I was to be killed in India.

It doesn't matter where you come from, where you are going, or who you do or don't hang with. It doesn't matter what you have done, who you have done it with, or how many times you've done it. God knows it all already, including everything you will do, and He has known since the foundations of the earth. Heterosexual, homosexual, adulterer, thief, murderer, liar, divorced, Jesus freak, worn and weary, in the valley or on the mountaintop, tomboy or girly-girl, rich or poor, single, married, in a picture-perfect family or not—God loves us and wants a personal relationship with all of us. Our sin has nothing to do with God's love for us. At the foot of the cross, we are all on the same level. We need to put down the stones and be led by the Spirit to exhort, encourage, and correct each other.

God's love is for everyone in the world, and He wants all to come into relationship with Him.

For God so loved the world that He gave His only begotten Son, that whoever believes in Him should not perish but have everlasting life (John 3:16, NKJV).

Relationship involves dialogue, and He wants to dialogue with us, to tell us what's coming, and to tell us about the destiny He planned before we were a glint in anyone's eye. Those plans involve powerful abilities. Those plans in-

There Is More

volve abundant living. Those plans involve a ridiculous freedom that can be explained only as supernatural.

What the Lord revealed to those soldiers was His Secret Service, the APTF: Angelic Protection Task Force. What happened with the soldiers is just one of the many encounters we had during that first trip to India. To explain everything that happened in the two weeks I was there would take a trilogy. And those are just my experiences abroad, not stateside. This kind of testimony comes from thousands of believers all over the world.

God is a consuming fire, chasing all of us to come into relationship with Him. His heart burns with the desire for our hearts to burn for Him. So, Fire chases fire in the hope that our flames turn toward and become one with His. Being a Christian is more than sitting in a pew and writing a check. There is more waiting for you! And it begins with the voice of God.

Two

Your Name

There was no alarm—just Him.

At the sound of His voice, I always immediately woke up at 5:30 a.m. On Sunday mornings I jumped out of bed to get ready to serve. At age ten, I had joined the Joy Bus Ministry of my church. Saturday mornings were dedicated to door-to-door invitations for children to take the bus to church. Sunday mornings began early with breakfast at the church before we rolled out all over the city to pick up and bring children to church.

These joyous and fruitful times slowly faded as I turned to a broader path. Even when I was in the midst of unwise choices, the voice of the Lord came to me—unsolicited, far from my mind. He was there. He never left.

It was 1989, my sophomore year at a college. One day when I was driving home on a country road, the Creator spoke, "Lisa."

It wasn't the faint whisper of ghosts portrayed in

movies. The voice was quiet peace radiating through my being and resounding in my brain. There was nothing before. Every cell in my body came to attention at the sound of His voice. My hands gripped the steering wheel. I felt as if a stranger had walked in the room, and I didn't want Him to discover me. Stillness came over me, and I was found.

There it was again—my name. Startled like a child unexpectedly caught by a parent, I gasped. There was no mistaking who it was. I felt frozen; my mind held only one thought. I knew that voice was God's.

I grew up in the church and was raised on Christian principles. However, by the time I got to college, I had stopped reading the Word and going to church. So why was God calling my name?

I took my right hand off the steering wheel and switched on the radio. To my amazement, somehow my radio was on a Christian station. The voice of some preacher came through my speakers. "God is calling YOU!"

Freaked out, I stared through my windshield as I drove. I jumped at another sound: my pager. Racing home with eternal fear, I just wanted to call my friend Michelle, who had paged me. Before fully braking in my driveway, I threw the car into park, pulled the brake, and ran in the house to my room to call her. "Girl! You are not going to believe what just happened to me." After a quick pause for composure, I told her, "God just called me."

"Girlfriend, you are trippin'. What's God going to do with a party girl? Send you to the club?"

Chasing Fire

We both started laughing and cracking jokes about it. Quickly the conversation changed to weekend plans.

I wonder how many of us have experienced this. How many of us have heard a command or direction, ever so slightly, only to turn around and find no one there? Whether we attend church or not, the Lord will speak. At the time the Lord whispered my name, I was not attending church. God was not on my radar at all. But I was on His.

The Most High called me. Not only did I dismiss Him, I laughed at His reach for me. If I had known everything that would happen in the next few years, I would have heeded His voice, and my response would have been quite different.

Is He reaching for you? Have you seen His arm of protection from death, disease, or calamity? Has your radio ever been tuned to a station you swear you did not put it on? Do questions pull at your heart, although you would never ask or even think them? If so, reach back toward Him. Don't do what I did. I ignored Him and continued my life of partying. By the time I was twenty-two years old, I had no evidence of salvation. I was far from the Lord and headed for the pigpen.

Too bad I didn't listen. Some people believe that once you are saved, you are always saved. Well, if I had died and met the Savior during the time I was friends with the world, it would not have astonished me if the Lord did not let me through the pearly gates.

Fast forward to years later, after my rededication to the Lord. I participated in a retreat activity that was emotional for everyone. A long checklist of sins was given to each person. We were to check the box next to the sins we had committed and then nail them to a cross.

This list brought an acute awareness of my sinful nature and how far I had strayed from God's commandments throughout my life. I checked off a lot of boxes! Anyway, it took the enemy only three years to put me into a pit of despair. Even though I had money, friends, success in school, and what I then thought was fun, I was depressed and had no hope.

But hallelujah! I am back in the fold, on the narrow road, and headed for home. I know who I am in Christ and am beginning to understand the destiny the Lord has for me as a sojourner. After all my experiences with God, you would think I would be good at submitting to what He says. I am not. Like you, I live in the world and have a constant battle with my flesh and the evil one. None of us is perfect. In the midst of our imperfection is a holy God, reaching down with His voice to spare us from consequences that come from poor decision-making. The great thing is that if we disobey or ignore His voice the way I did, the reach from heaven's throne does not cease. His hand is always there, just waiting for us to grab it.

While driving that day, I saw no sudden, ominous cloud spreading across the horizon with lightning bolts accompanied by a voice like James Earl Jones. I was not caught up into heaven like John the Revelator or struck down like Paul on the road to Damascus. In His infinite wisdom, God chose to whisper my name—a name with no titles before or letters behind it—just a nineteen-year-old girl He sent His Son to die for.

Chasing Fire

That same death was for you. God knows our names. The Bible tells us that He knew us before he laid down the foundations of the earth. It only makes sense that when He speaks to us, He would address us by name. This is demonstrated all through scripture. Below are some examples.

Then the Lord said to Cain, "Where is Abel your brother?" He said, "I do not know. Am I my brother's keeper?" (Genesis 4:9, NKJV)

And He said, "Hagar, Sarai's maid, where have you come from, and where are you going?" She said, "I am fleeing from the presence of my mistress Sarai" (Genesis 16:8, NKJV).

And the Lord said to Abraham, "Why did Sarah laugh, saying, 'Shall I surely bear a child, since I am old?'" (Genesis 18:13, NKJV)

So when the Lord saw that he turned aside to look, God called to him from the midst of the bush and said, "Moses, Moses!" And he said, "Here I am" (Exodus 3:4, NKJV).

Now the Lord came and stood and called as at other times, "Samuel! Samuel!" And Samuel answered, "Speak, for Your servant hears" (1 Samuel 3:10, NKJV).

Now there was a certain disciple at Damascus named Ananias; and to him the Lord said in a vision,

Your Name

"Ananias." And he said, "Here I am, Lord" (Acts 9:10, NKJV).

As they ministered to the Lord and fasted, the Holy Spirit said, "Now separate to Me Barnabas and Saul for the work to which I have called them" (Acts 13:2, NKJV).

God calls us by name because names are important. Names are written in the Book of Life. Next to our name might be a reference number to our deeds that are documented in other books.

Your eyes saw my substance, being yet unformed. And in Your book they all were written, the days fashioned for me, when as yet there were none of them (Psalm 139:16, NKJV).

And I saw the dead, small and great, standing before God, and books were opened. And another book was opened, which is the Book of Life. And the dead were judged according to their works, by the things which were written in the books (Revelation 20:12, NKJV).

Our names have meaning that is tied to our destiny and purpose. When the Lord speaks our name, He is not only addressing our identification but also the destiny and plan attached to us according to Jeremiah.

Chasing Fire

"For I know the plans that I have for you," declares the Lord, "plans for welfare and not for calamity to give you a future and a hope" (Jeremiah 29:11, NASB).

Some of us may not have heard the Lord call our name. Remember a time when you were minding your own business, doing what you needed to do, and suddenly your mom, dad, or boss came to you and said in a frustrated voice, "Didn't you hear me calling you?"

The same thing happens with God. We are so busy doing what we feel needs to be done that we don't even hear Him. We have tuned in to so many things, including static, that the Lord's voice is muffled or not heard at all. Work, school, family, children, clubs, sports, the Internet, movies, television, radio programs, parties, and even church activities compete for our time. These things are not inherently evil, but they keep us from the One who protects us from evil. Sitting in silence to hear the Creator of the Universe is last on the list—if it is on the list at all.

Anything we do or say that glorifies sin and/or brings us into temptation is static. It separates us from clear direction and puts us on a path that separates us from God. Eventually, our antenna receives direction from the world, and we don't hear the voice of God because our spirits are tuned in to the wrong station. Clear communication is challenging in the natural, so we have to be adamant in hearing spiritually. We have to make a decision to keep God as our focus.

In high school, I had the privilege of playing on a championship basketball team. We won our league championship every year and went to the playoffs for our conference championship. One year, we won C.I.F. and went to the playoffs for the state championship. The reason our team was successful was because we chose to listen to our coach. It didn't matter how loud the crowd was. I never knew what was happening in the stands or even on the bench. Through all the noise and commotion, the voice I never missed was that of my coach.

Think about it. He had no microphone. He spoke to us from a sitting position. If he stood up, someone was in trouble or he had something important to get to us, usually by a hand signal so no one else would know what he was saying. He could call a play with a facial expression or wave of his hand. Sometimes we could anticipate what he would say in practice, half-time, time out, or on the court. We knew him and his voice.

But no wonder. We were with him a lot! We practiced for two or three hours, Monday through Friday. Games were twice a week, and we traveled to tournaments. We participated in summer season, pre-season, and the regular season, so I played basketball from July through May. I was with my coach and teammates all the time. I spent more time with my coach than my own family and close friends.

God is our Life Coach. In order to hear Him call us and give us the plays for success, we have to spend time with Him. We have to read and get to know His playbook, which is His Word, the Bible. He has to take up the majority of our time. Making Him our focus allows us to live in a chaotic, noisy world and one day win His trophy with our name on it.

Chasing Fire

I'd like to give you a challenge. Go to a quiet place and call upon Him. Then sit alone in silence for an hour and wait on the Lord. Don't do dishes, don't play music, and don't walk around. Just sit in silence with your heart pressed toward heaven. God promises in Jeremiah:

Call to Me, and I will answer you, and show you great and mighty things, which you do not know (Jeremiah 33:3 NKJV).

Now when you do this, some things might happen. Feelings of nervousness or anxiousness may arise. These could be signs that He is on the way. Continue to press on and call out to Him. Some of us will all of a sudden have hunger pains, the phone may ring, or we'll start thinking about things that we need to do. This is the devil trying to change your focus because he wants you bound and bored rather than found and soaring.

Keep calling to God. An awesome stillness or a peaceful silence might come into the room. That's Him. Tears may fall. That's Him. If tears turn to talking and confessing to Him, He has arrived. Feelings of warmth, protection, and extreme peace are indications that He is there. The bottom line is this: if you are sincere and truly want to hear the Lord and you call out to Him for an hour, He will show up.

One of the most wonderful things about our God is His unlimited forgiveness. If we ever ignore His voice or call, He is quick to forgive and give us another chance. As long as we are living on the earth, we serve the God of innumerable chances. The blood of Jesus is a perpetual, eternal flow that covers everything that's done, being done, and will be done. Praise God! The Lord will continually call to us. He already sent His Son to the cross. What's talking to you?

Maybe you wonder who you are. Well, you are a soul that was purchased at Calvary. You were knit in a womb crafted by the hand of the Lord. You are someone God loves and with whom God wants to have a relationship. That means you can have back-and-forth dialogue. God sits on the throne and resides in heaven. This is true. He is also the omnipresent God we call Abba, Daddy.

For you did not receive the spirit of bondage again to fear, but you received the Spirit of adoption by whom we cry out, "Abba, Father" (Romans 8:15 NKJV).

No dad on the planet has anything on the Maker of our soul. No kingdom on earth has the benefits His Kingdom has in eternity. The Queen of England has a kingdom, but not all her citizens are royalty. In God's Kingdom, all citizens are deemed His children, His heirs, and sit at the right hand of His Son. The citizens of England have no access to the queen unless they are special. But every person on the planet has access to the Creator of the Universe, and an appointment is not necessary. He is all-powerful and all-knowing, hears all our prayers all the time, can answer prayers simultaneously, and will miraculously give each hearer His undivided attention. His mercy, grace, and love abound, but He will always bring justice to life circumstances. He is perfect.

Chasing Fire

The Spirit Himself bears witness with our spirit that we are children of God, and if children, then heirs— heirs of God and joint heirs with Christ, if indeed we suffer with Him, that we may also be glorified together (Romans 8:16-17, NKJV).

But God, who is rich in mercy, because of His great love with which He loved us, even when we were dead in trespasses, made us alive together with Christ (by grace you have been saved), and raised us up together, and made us sit together in the heavenly places in Christ Jesus (Ephesians 2:4-6, NKJV).

But you are a chosen generation, a royal priesthood, a holy nation, His own special people, that you may proclaim the praises of Him who called you out of darkness into His marvelous light; who once were not a people but are now the people of God, who had not obtained mercy but now have obtained mercy (1 Peter 2:9-10, NKJV).

The perfect dad talks with his children. God wants to talk with you. He wants to bless us. It is almost ridiculous, considering how holy He is and how imperfect we are. Still, He wants us all to live abundantly. We cannot attain the abundant life without His wisdom and direction. This requires hearing Him and knowing His voice.

You may already hear the Lord. You have a smashing relationship with God. You walk with Him, talk with Him, and live an abundant life. You see His hand in your life and acknowledge the mighty things He has revealed to you in your time with Him. You know beyond a shadow of a doubt that His Word is true. You are a witness to His joy when you should have none, His mercy when you should have a consequence, and His grace when you should be condemned. You attend church and you serve, but you are quiet. No one knows your testimony. You have not told those in your sphere of influence how awesome the Lord has been to you or shared the wonderful conversations you have had with Him.

Be encouraged. You are not alone in hearing God. I know it's hard to say things like "the Lord told me," unless you are Billy Graham, T.D. Jakes, Joyce Meyer, Beth Moore, or some other nationally known Christian. The media and some churches have placed a stigma on people who say they hear God. This makes it challenging to discuss our conversations with Him. How sad. How can a lost world come to a God that no one or only a select few are able to hear?

If you are one who hears, talk about it. Share your prayer needs and then the answer the Lord brings. If the Lord is asking you to make a change in your life, tell people about it. Tell them the special things you are asking God for, and when He brings them, show everyone.

Tim Tebow, a former NFL quarterback, is doing a great job of living out his relationship with God, openly and with humility. The entire world knows and sees the hand of God in his life. His actions have been the same throughout his life but have recently become known because the Lord has put him on a world stage.

Chasing Fire

Another example of someone who is living their life for the Lord and reaping blessing is you! So share it. Everyone is coming out of the closet these days. Come out of the Christian closet. Be bold. God has your back. We should not fear what we could lose. Paul proclaims in Romans:

> *For I am not ashamed of the gospel, for it is the power of God for salvation to everyone who believes, to the Jews first and also to the Greek* (Romans 1:16, NASB)

I don't know why the Lord chose us to reap a harvest for His Kingdom. But He did. That means we must share our knowledge of Him with others.

Some of us have heard the Lord, others have ignored Him, and some have tuned Him out. Some may not even believe in God or that He speaks to men today. It doesn't matter who you are, what your religious beliefs are, or what your spiritual experiences have been. The truth is that whether or not you call on His name, He knows yours. The Lord Jesus teaches in John:

> *But he who enters by the door is the shepherd of the sheep. To him the doorkeeper opens, and the sheep hear His voice; and He calls His own sheep by name and leads them out. I am the good shepherd; and I know My sheep, and am known by my own* (John 10:2-3, 14, NKJV).

One of the first things we learn about someone we meet is their name. It is the beginning of what will connect us with that person. The next time we see the person, we call them by their name. They may not recognize our voice, but they turn when they realize that someone knows who they are. The fact that God knows our name establishes that He knows who we are. In fact, He knows everything about us. No matter who you are, God speaks, and He wants you to hear Him.

Three

His Presence

My act was award-winning. Drowning in despair, I successfully and masterfully cloaked myself in the appearance of perfect happiness. My friends had no idea I was plagued with thoughts no one should have. They were completely unaware of my depression.

Why? Because according to the world's standards, I had no reason to be depressed. I did not have the reason myself. Everything was going great. I was about to graduate with a major published work. I took second at the Collegiate State Competition for Persuasive Speaking. I was a successful journalist for our college paper, popular, and (if you don't mind me saying so) pretty. What was causing the darkness in me? I had no answer.

The summer before my senior year, I went home. My dad offered me an opportunity I could not refuse. "Listen, after you graduate, you will work for the rest of your life. Take it easy this summer. Here is a membership to the gym, and I will give you an allowance. All you have to do is

His Presence

take your sister to school and pick her up when we need you to and keep the downstairs clean."

Cha-ching! It was on. I was ready to keep the party going. I called all my friends. We went to the beach, sailing, to parties of the rich and famous, and, of course, dancing at the clubs. Everything was awesome until I rubbed my sister Danielle the wrong way.

She was saved, sanctified, and had already served on the mission field in Fiji and India with YWAM (Youth With A Mission). My presence, I am sure, was an agitation. I came out of my room getting ready to go out, and she rebuked me for the way I was dressed. Now I know she was right to do so.

We did not have much to say after that until I heard one of her music tapes by Rachel Rachel, a contemporary Christian female rock duo. The music on this tape had the power of the Pied Piper of the classic fairy tale, "The Pied Piper of Hamelin" by Robert Browning, Johann Wolfgang von Goethe, and the Brothers Grimm. Each time I heard it, I was physically drawn to my sister's closed bedroom door. Many times I made my way to her room. Since her frustration with me was louder than a freight train moving at full speed, I figured there was no way she would allow me to borrow it. Yet the draw became stronger and stronger until one day I asked her to let me use it. She agreed and immediately handed the tape to me.

That was a totally unexpected response. I understand it now. God is sneaky. I had heard that tape many times from my sister's room, but this time it was different. The tunes these ladies played were taking me to a type of death, a sure

Chasing Fire

destruction. And the One playing through them came with a sword that would slay the darkness in me on that day. A funeral was coming, but a resurrection was on the way. I would soon be revived!

When the house was empty, I began my chores and started the tape. At the first note of the first song, the atmosphere of the family room changed. Someone entered unseen but firmly present. I sat on the couch and listened to every word of every lyric of every song. By the end of the last song, I was weeping as this band sang out my current life and feelings.

When the tape stopped, I realized my sin. A split second later, a heavy weight filled the air. The weight caused me to fall from the couch to my knees into a crawling position.

God's silent presence was the loudest thing I'd ever experienced. He didn't need words; He used that music tape. Then He made His presence known to me. He was there all along. There I was stripped, completely naked. He knew everything and opened my closet for all the skeletons to fall out.

Suddenly I was acutely aware of the One who sees. For me, this was an opportunity to confess and be forgiven and set free from the despair and depression I was plagued with. No one knew but Him. My God saw. He was there.

I had not prayed in years. I sobbed uncontrollably as my eyes poured water like a released dam. The only words from my mouth were confession and repentance before the Great High Priest. Then the weight lifted and so did my head. The unseen presence remaining in my family room was a supernatural peace surrounded with authority and love.

His Presence

I was struck with a reverent fear. It was like being sent to a principal's office for disobeying and waiting to know what the outcome would be, only exponentially worse. I got back up on the couch and sat quietly waiting to see what He would do. This time I was not going to turn on the radio. I asked with respectful reference, "Now what?"

Some of my most enjoyable years working in the early childhood field were times I taught two-year-olds. My classroom was orderly and clean. My curriculum proved successful, but above all those things, my children were cared for and loved. The physical environment was set up in a way that allowed me to see everything most of the time. Very little escaped me. One day a child was in a corner at the front of the classroom, looking at a book. After a few minutes, another child came over and took the book. The first child yelled, "Mine!" and snatched the book back. At that moment, the other child pushed the one with the book.

I went over and engaged in a practice that allows both children to learn instead of just rectifying the situation with swift consequences. "What happened?" I asked the second child. "Your friend is crying."

Pushed child: "He pushed me."

Me to child who pushed: "Why did you push your friend?"

Child who pushed: "He took my book!"

Pushed child: "No! It's my book!"

Me to child who pushed: "Who was reading the book first?"

Child who pushed: "Me."

Both children continued to yell and claim they had it first. I recapped what happened. The child who pushed tried to convince me he had the book first.

"You did not have the book first," I said. "You came over from the block area and took the book out of your friend's hands."

Before he could continue his argument I continued, "I saw you."

Sarai convinced her husband, Abram, to sleep with Hagar, the maidservant, in order to produce the promised son of God. Though this was not God's plan, Abram agreed, and Hagar became pregnant. Jealousy rose in Sarai's heart and pride in Hagar's. Sarai treated Hagar so badly that Hagar left. The Angel of the Lord (many scholars believe this to be the Lord Himself) met her at a well and asked where she was going. After she shared her ordeal with Him, he gave her some promises and told her to go back. In Genesis 16:13, she called the Lord "You-Are-The-God-Who-Sees" and stated, "Have I also here seen Him who sees me?" (NKJV)

Our God sees. He has the all-seeing eye that never slumbers or sleeps. His watch never ceases. Nothing occurs on earth or in the universe that He does not see, including you. If His eye is seeing, then He is ever present. He's there while we are awake, while we are sleeping, when we are making wise decisions, and when we are not. He sees us fall, get up, fail, and succeed. He sees because He is there.

So why does God ask questions He should already have

His Presence

the answers to if He sees and is there? It could be the same reason we ask similar questions of our children, students, protégés, employees, or anyone who receives leadership from us. We already have the answers. But this creates an opportunity for the other person to learn, to confess, to be forgiven, to be restored, and to bring healing, justice, and many other eternal blessings.

In Acts 3:19, we are told to repent and convert that our sins may be blotted out and times of refreshing may come from the presence of the Lord. He has seen everything that has happened to us and to others by us. He saw the thievery. He saw the murder. He sees when our hearts get broken. He sees when our dreams blow up in our faces. He sees when we lose a job and when others gossip about us, lie about us, slander us, and cheat on us. He sees all the injustice we have endured. Beloved, He also sees the ones we inflict on others.

We are all a stolen-book-from-a-classmate away from salvation. God has provided a way to Him. We need only to receive it. Some of us tell everybody else what we do and/or have done. Tell the Lord. You can be assured that, unlike those we take confidence in, He will not repeat the matter, not even to you. God promises in the Psalms,

As far as the east is from the west, so far has He removed our transgressions from us (Psalm 103:12, NKJV).

Once the sin is forgiven, the words from the cross resonate in our soul, "It is finished."

It's over. There is no condemnation. Grace and mercy

abound and the Lord bestows upon us His patience and compassion. His love is relentless. Our mighty God (who keeps track of the hairs on our head) cares for each of us. His love for us is so obsessive, there is nothing we can do that the blood can't eradicate. Let me quote Beth Moore: "I know. I'm living proof."

On the couch, waiting for a verdict, I heard no response. All I heard was a continued deafening, silent peace. I know a worship song about the sweet presence of Jesus. In my walk, I have experienced the sweetness. This was not one of those times.

I was in trouble. I sat there wondering if I should get up and finish my chores or just sit there and wait. One thing I was thankful for—He gave me another chance to respond. I was hardheaded the first time, so He used a different angle. It worked. Recounting this event in my life reminds me of another verse:

> *But He is unique, and who can make Him change? And whatever His soul desires, that He does. For He performs what is appointed for me and many such things are with Him. Therefore I am terrified at His presence, when I consider this, I am afraid* (Job 23:13-15, NKJV).

Your appointment is coming. He's the Father, so there won't be only one. If you had one already, there is another on the books. If you haven't had one yet, cause Him to marvel like the centurion soldier mentioned in the gospels. Meet Him at the door.

When my sister came home, I told her that I gave my life back to the Lord, and I was going with her to church. I reconnected with fellow students from the Christian school I had attended and started to get to know Him and those who follow Him again. It was a great, new beginning. I was refreshed, free. My day of repentance was a day of deliverance. Despair and depression left; peace and joy came in. I did not see God or His Son with my eyes. I did not hear a voice. It was the clear communication of His presence that commanded the chains to be gone and my soul to be whole.

On one episode of the television show, "The Biggest Loser," the participants ran a race, carrying the weight they had lost up to that point of the competition. When each person was packed with the weight they had hauled for a lifetime, amazement and bewilderment showed on their faces. All were astonished at how heavy it was. It was almost unfathomable that the uncomfortable weight they were about to carry for the race was not a burden until they looked in the mirror or went shopping for clothes. This is how the weight of sin is. We do what we want to do and think it is no big deal until one day we look in the mirror and realize something has to change.

During a street ministry outreach, I encountered some college students who had come out of a bar. They were wasted—totally trashed. I approached them (two girls) and asked if I could get them a cab. They said no and asked if I were a Christian. When I said yes, they started to laugh about what a boring life I had and how I wasn't able to do anything "fun." They clearly thought I was bound and had no freedom.

Chasing Fire

I looked them straight in the eye, and the Holy Spirit came upon me with boldness. "I am free," I said. "You, on the other hand, have no choice but to come out here every weekend and give your mind over to alcohol and sometimes your body over to someone you don't know. The next morning, you wake up disgusted for a minute, but then you brush it off with acceptance by telling yourself this is just how it is."

That's how it is only if we choose to endure living that way. But it doesn't have to be. Can we be real for a moment? Who likes waking up in the morning to grab onto a toilet? If the "walk of shame" is funny, why is the word "shame" in the phrase? How does what happens in Vegas, stay in Vegas when the STD, the baby, and the gambling debt come home? Why do we continue to participate in things we don't like, things that don't make us feel fulfilled, and things that keep peace and joy out of our lives, not to mention bring harm and hurt to others? These things are chains that keep us bound and away from the true freedom we can have.

That freedom comes from Christ. John 8:36 says that if the Son makes you free you shall be free indeed. We are told in Psalm 107 of the distressed who cried out to the Lord. After they cried out, the Lord brought them out of darkness and the shadow of death and broke their chains in pieces.

His presence will lead us to repentance. His presence will lift our head and demand respect. His presence will set us free. And in the presence of the Lord, we will be protected.

His Presence

God made us exactly the way we are for a divine purpose. He will not let anything happen to us that would cause His plan to fail.

Not long ago, a chance called "death" visited a pastor's wife at my church. A car collision on a major highway resulted in praise, thanksgiving, and tears of joy instead of sadness and funeral preparations. Everyone walked away from the incident except her. After hospitalization, surgery, and rehabilitation, she walks and is able to enjoy life as though the accident never happened. All those involved in the accident need to be alive and physically functioning in order to complete what the Lord has for them to do on this earth.

He may allow others to remain disabled for the majority of their life, like the lame man at the temple gate called Beautiful. Lame from birth, he sat at this gate each day as a beggar. Though Jesus probably passed this man each time He went to the temple, He did not heal him. This man was not healed until after the resurrection, and then it was Peter whom God used to heal him (Acts 3:1-8).

Why didn't Jesus heal him? As a Jew, at least once a year for Passover, Jesus went to Jerusalem through the gate called Beautiful to enter the temple. Yet He did not heal him while He was on the earth. Why not?

When we were three or four years old, most of us made scribble marks on paper and then proudly showed it to our parents, exclaiming, "Look, Mommy and Daddy! I drew you!" Likewise, I am about to create a picture of how God moves.

Perhaps someone in Jesus' day needed to witness the

Chasing Fire

miracle of the lame man's healing, and maybe that person could not be at the gate until the exact day and precise time Peter and John walked by. Then this witness might have gone home and shared the story with people who may have not listened to it if it hadn't been for the timing. Maybe specific circumstances in their lives were not happening at the time Jesus was seeing the lame man at the Gate Beautiful. But the timing was right and they listened, taking the story to our ancestors in the right time. There could be a direct link between us and them, due to the timing. See how it works?

Our heavenly Father wants us to be in His presence. When Jesus breathed His last breath on the cross, the temple veil, dividing man from the glory of God, tore in half. We are reconciled to God through the blood of Jesus Christ. Jesus became the bridge to an intimate relationship with a perfect and holy God. We have access to Him and should seek to be in His presence. His eye is on the sparrow, and He watches over us all the time. Get this. Right now, God is looking at you. His presence is there. And maybe when you close this book it will be like the end of the music tape, and He will make His presence known.

Four

The Word

I wonder who closed the book right away at the end of the last chapter to see what happened and who turned the page quickly to keep on reading. It would be great to know what is being experienced or considered regarding God's voice. Keep in mind that we are talking about an eternal, spiritual entity who is obsessed with His creation. He will do and use anything to get your attention for the purpose of entering into a relationship with you. Remember, His fire is chasing ours.

He will use all kinds of events, people, circumstances, and media, like this book, to reach every soul. One book in particular that He uses to speak to us is the Bible. God has spoken directly into my immediate circumstances through the Holy Scriptures many times. Sometimes I turn the page quickly to escape what He is putting in my heart. Other times, I reflect and obey.

After graduation, I moved to the San Francisco Bay area. In Judges 4, we read about the prophetess Deborah, a

Chasing Fire

judge over Israel, who fulfilled her role sitting under a tree. I was no judge, but there I was, sitting under a tree, crying out to God for help. Even though I had rededicated my life the summer before my senior year, I'm sure my Christian walk resembled the gait of a drunken person. I stumbled, fell, bumped into others, and had blurred vision and slurred speech. I was a baby trying to run and couldn't even crawl. I was a mess. Anyway, I made it out of my Egypt and cried out for a church home and Christian fellowship.

This prayer was answered swiftly. In the midst of my plea, before an "Amen," my attention was grabbed by the blow of a car horn. A brother in the Lord asked me a question. In the brief dialogue, I both answered his questions and received my own answer. At the sound of the church name he attended, my ears received a message that translated as a call in my heart. It beat with purpose, and so I went.

A Vineyard Christian Fellowship in the East Bay area became my church home. The embrace of the people there was a hug so powerful, I still feel it today. They helped me embark on a magnificent journey that began with a love for worshipping the Lord and for God's Word. I was filled with joy and expectant of destiny. My fire caught Fire.

Excited about the Lord and anxious to know Him more, I became obsessed with the Bible. It was my American Express card—I never left home without it. The Word remained with me throughout the day. On the way to work, I would read the Word; during breaks and lunch, I would read it. If my time was not occupied doing something else, I was reading God's Word.

The Word

Further, they argue that one of the signs of the end times is that people will be lovers of themselves.

> *But know this, that in the last days perilous times will come: For men will be lovers of themselves, lovers of money, boasters, proud, blasphemers, disobedient to parents, unthankful, unholy, unloving, unforgiving, slanderers, without self-control, brutal, despisers of good, traitors, headstrong, haughty, lovers of pleasure rather than lovers of God, having a form of godliness but denying its power. And from such people turn away!* (2 Timothy 3:1-5, NKJV)

After studying these verses from the Greek, I made a discovery. In Matthew, the phrase "love your neighbor as yourself" is translated using three words: *Agapao* (love) meaning an unconditional, general acceptance and care; *plesion* (thy neighbor) meaning every person outside of yourself; and *seautou* (yourself) meaning you. In 2 Timothy 3:2, the phrase "lovers of themselves" is translated using one word: *phliautos*, meaning too intent on your own interest; selfish. Loving your neighbor as yourself and being a lover of yourself are two different concepts. The first deals with the individual person and the latter with the person's interest.

When a person has an unconditional acceptance and care for who they are (good and bad), what they are capable of (good and bad), and why they are, the eyes of the soul are opened to see others in a different light. Knowing our own weaknesses allows us to give grace to the weaknesses of others. Recognizing our wrongdoings allows us to forgive and be merciful. Being excited about and wholeheartedly embracing our destiny prevents comparison, competitiveness, and jealousy. Understanding that we need help with no strings attached enables us to serve and give without expecting anything in return. Loving others has to begin with loving ourselves.

God calls us to love ourselves in order to accept and lay hold of everything He has made us to be and do. We live in a fallen, mean world. It is a world filled with people who hurt us with words and deeds specifically designed to incite low self-esteem. Again, this type of acceptance of self is not conceit, pride, or arrogance. It is a healthy sense of self and self-worth, a positive self-concept.

Your self-worth and self-esteem come directly from the way you think about yourself. If self-assessments such as, "I am stupid," "I am unlovable," "I am weak," "I have no power," "I am ugly," or "I am unable, I can't" outweigh positive self-assessments, the result is low self-worth and low self-esteem. People who have low self-worth and low self-esteem have a difficult time receiving great things because they don't believe they are worthy of them. Their brain has been wired to receive only the things that align with their self-assessment.

As an Infant-Toddler Specialist in California, my knowledge increased regarding identity formation and the importance of having a positive self concept for success. If your self-assessments lead to the belief that you are not valued, it is difficult to receive all the positive attributes the Lord has placed in our character and personality, as well as

The Word

the wonderful blessings He has for us here and now, while we are living on Earth. God wants us to have a healthy self-concept, self-worth and self-esteem. He wants us to embrace and walk out the identity He has given through Christ. So what is this identity? Here are some attributes outlined in God's Word:

- You have the mind of Christ (1 Corinthians 2:16)
- You are a royal priesthood (1 Peter 2:9)
- You have supernatural gifts to be used for blessing others (1 Corinthians 12:4-31)
- You have supernatural power and authority to cast out evil spirits that afflict you and others (Matthew 10:1, Mark 6:7, Luke 10:19-20)

The above are only four attributes—promises given to those who have received Christ. There are more. But do you believe it? When you look in the mirror, do you see royalty, a healer, or worker of miracles? Whom do you see? Does it match who God says you are? If not, the Lord has provided a solution. He has the ability to rewire our thinking.

If we ever feel unworthy, unloved, or rejected, or if we believe nothing good can happen for us, these feelings are real. We should not ignore them or deny them. We must trust the Creator and give Him a chance to exchange them. He is all-powerful. In His omnipotent way, He uses the truth of His Word to destroy the lying thought processes meant to destroy our soul.

Chasing Fire

You are worthy. You are loved. You are accepted. And God has great things in store for you. These truths are repeatedly outlined in His Word. In it is the power to renew our mind, heal our spirit, and change our feelings about ourselves. God wants us to have a healthy self-concept so we can have the confidence to accomplish His plan successfully. He wants us to receive all that He has for us and believe what He thinks about us. Embracing and living out the identity He gives us is the key to having positive thoughts and responses. Then we can gain a deeper understanding of others. Our view is widened with an eternal lens. We see more. This is the secret to living out 1 John 4:7-8, which calls us to love one another with the love of God and love our neighbor as ourselves. God also commands this in Leviticus, Matthew, Romans, Galatians, and James.

All the rules in the Bible are based on love for the Lord, yourself, and your neighbor. If everyone was serious about taking care of their physical bodies, keeping their soul intact and recognizing the importance of others doing the same, sexual promiscuity would not be so rampant. If every person living, both now and in the future, committed to abstain from sex until marriage and stay with that person through thick and thin and not have another, sexually transmitted diseases would be greatly diminished within two generations. In addition, families would not be broken up, and more hearts would remain intact.

God's rules are like a parent warning a baby not to touch a hot stove. God knows the dangerous things that can hurt us and others. He wants us to be safe. He wants us

The Word

to be healthy. He wants to bless us with joy and peace. And He has left the bestseller of all time so we can learn how to receive those things. All we have to do is read it, believe it, and implement it.

Do I believe that all humanity began with Adam and Eve? Yes. Do I believe that God chose to flood the earth, sparing one family? Yes. Do I believe that the walls of Jericho came tumbling down by the blow of trumpets? Yes. Do I believe that Jonah survived being eaten alive by a whale and then regurgitated after three days? Yes. Do I believe that three young men were thrown into a fiery furnace and not burned or harmed at all? Yes, I do. Do I believe that Jesus was born of a virgin, turned water to wine, healed the sick, raised the dead, then raised Himself from the grave and came to His disciples by walking through a wall? Absolutely! And I believe He is coming back.

The historical record of God's relationship with people is for our encouragement. It is also there to let us know exactly who we are dealing with. The things listed above seem farfetched to many because they are impossible for us. We know these are things men cannot do. They are miraculous, supernatural.

Life existing due to an explosion is easier for the mind to accept than the verses "Let there be ... and there was." It's easier because if the theory of a highly unlikely accidental explosion is true, then there will probably not be another one that can create more life for us to compete with. And that also means there is no one who can take us all out. We don't have to respond. We can continue in our own way without accountability. "Let there be ... and there was"

Chasing Fire

is entirely different. Accepting this Bible teaching as truth means Someone did this—on purpose. It tells us that all things are possible with Him (Matthew 19:26).

I have studied how the scrolls were combined into the canonized Bible and how they were written in different continents over thousands of years by people who never met each other. Yet they say the same thing. I also saw the Dead Sea Scrolls in Jerusalem. I am more than convinced that the Bible is the Word of God, breathed by the Holy Spirit through the vessels He chose to pen it. It comes down to faith. You're either going to believe it or you're not. But here is another challenge. Read the Bible for yourself, from cover to cover, like any other book. Research the history of the Bible and its characters in an attempt to disprove its contents. I promise that you will be surprised at your findings.

It's simple: God loves you and you need to have faith in that Love. God loves each of you so much that He stays awake for eternity with the most intimate details of your life on His mind. He wants to give you a future and a hope (Jeremiah 29:11). He wants you to have an abundant life (John 10:10). He wants to prosper the work of your hands (Psalm 1:3). And He wants you to be healthy (1 Corinthians 6:19).

Hearing that my body was a temple, I became keenly aware of what happened the last time I did not listen. What to do was a no-brainer. I immediately put the cigarette out and threw my pack away. Thank God I hadn't smoked so long that it was an addiction. I've known people who love the Lord but have struggled to stop smoking for years. Like

The Word

Paul, they absolutely hate the habit and are fighting to stop. "For the good that I will to do, I do not do; but the evil I will not to do, that I practice" (Romans 7:19, NKJV).

But hallelujah! My eyes have also seen people completely set free. God's Word is alive!

For the word of God is living and powerful, and sharper than any two-edged sword, piercing even to the division of soul and spirit, and of joints and marrow, and is a discerner of the thoughts and intents of the heart (Hebrews 4:12, NKJV).

He uses the Word to speak to our circumstances, teach, convict, and comfort us. His Word tests, heals, and exhorts us. We have it as a weapon and as a light to our path. It renews our mind. We can depend on God's Word. It never fails and will never pass away.

When God speaks to me through His Word, it makes me crave more. Does He read it to me out loud every time I open it? No. When He does, I receive it, even when I don't like what He is saying. Honestly, there are things in the Word that I don't like. However, truth is truth, whether you like it or not. God's Word is a map to our success in this life and the hereafter. We need it to know Him and His ways more. He is Almighty God. It's His Word and it's accurate—pure truth. So, I trust and obey … most of the time.

Five

Correction From a Brotha'

Growing up in my parents' home, I became a witness to giving. My parents gave a lot of their time, funds, and even our home to people who needed it. Unfortunately, I was not a witness to their discussions about boundaries on their giving. Nor was I privy to any conversations they may have had with the individuals receiving their assistance. Were there boundaries? Was there a plan? I didn't know. All I saw were people coming and going. So I thought that whenever someone needed a place to stay, it was an automatic yes. There was no need to pray about it or ask questions about their life. After all, the Word says if you have, you should give, right?

So I gave my apartment or should I say I shared my apartment. Although I had known her for only a short time, I allowed a young woman, Ellie, to stay with me. Only a week had gone by when people I trusted began to ask questions. Who was Ellie? How did I know her? What was her plan? How long was she going to stay? Where was

Correction From a Brotha'

her family? Where was she from? What did she do for a living?

I only knew three things about Ellie: her name, the fact that she had a daughter in Florida, and the fact she was in Austin to win the love of a boyfriend who'd broken up with her.

This information raised my friends' eyebrows even higher. They started asking me about the daughter. Why were they not together? I didn't know. Therefore, I asked her for more information about her life circumstances, and she told me her story.

After listening to their concerns about my new roommate, instead of praying about it first (like I should have), I talked to her. She was a hairdresser, she said, and would be getting a position soon that would allow her to move in few weeks. When I asked about her daughter, she said she missed her but had to get things settled here in Austin before she could send for her. In the midst of all this, her heart was yearning for her ex-boyfriend.

Most of her conversation was about him. It wasn't focused on her job search or her plan to see her daughter. This started to put a load on my heart. Talking to her became draining, and my peace and joy soon deflated.

When I told my friends about Ellie's drama, they asked me to pray about my role and whether it was God's best for her to stay with me until … whenever. My girlfriends told me very sweetly, "Sister, it is time for her to go. She needs to be with her daughter."

But how do you kick a heartbroken woman out of your

Chasing Fire

home? I did not want to add to the sting of lost love.

Recently, my husband and I attended a seminar hosted by *Reasons to Believe*, a ministry that brings in speakers to provide scientific knowledge to believers regarding the existence of God. The seminar was titled, "The Theology of the String Theory: The Biblical Implications of Extra Dimensionality."

In a nutshell, the string theory suggests that the universe is made of vibrating strands of energy called strings instead of a point particle. For the theory to be legitimate, there must be more dimensions than the four we are currently aware of. In fact, there must be at least eleven. The speaker explained that this scientific theory of extra-dimensionality can help us make sense of God being triune, Jesus being both man and God, dead and then alive and able to walk through walls.

It is exciting to see scientists making discoveries that lead to God. However, despite all our present knowledge and the knowledge to come, the scriptures are clear. God's ways are higher than ours, and we will never fully understand Him or His ways while on this earth.

For as the heavens are higher than the earth, so are My ways higher than your ways, and My thoughts than your thoughts (Isaiah 55:9, NASB).

Great is our Lord and abundant in strength; His understanding is infinite (Psalm 147:5, NASB).

As described in the book *Flatland* by Edwin A. Abbot,

we live in a dimension that does not allow us to see the full picture. I didn't know God's plan for this woman. Knowledge of my entire future was far from me. God had only just begun speaking to me about my current situation. Having unanswered questions in my own life, I was crippled in understanding what the Lord had in store for the guest in my home. Finally I decided to seek the Lord and asked Him for a sign that would tell me what to do. The sign came through my friend Josh.

Josh is a happy guy. He is usually smiling, enjoys his company, and always has something positive to say. Up to this point, I had never seen or heard him behave any other way. One day, while visiting him and his roommate, John, I received a phone call from Ellie. I listened as, once again, she talked about everything but her plans. The one-sided conversation ended. I hung up the phone.

"Lisa!" Josh stood over me with his arms crossed over his chest. "Look at what just happened! When you came in here, you were filled with light. Then you got on the phone with that woman for two minutes, and your energy and peace were gone. I know you care for her, but it's time to let her go."

What just happened to him? He wasn't smiling, and fire blazed from his eyes. He shook his head and stalked into the kitchen.

His roommate, John, said with a smile, "You know he's right."

And he was.

Good intentions are not always God's intentions. My

Chasing Fire

intentions for my new friend were good, but they were getting in the way of God's best. As finite beings, we can't always see God's best. When we help others without knowing God's will, we can unintentionally become their god and keep them from their destiny and role on earth. Dependence on us becomes their expectation and our burden. When we enable people, we can move them from being helped to being helpless in fulfilling the call of the One who made them.

Giving to the poor, helping the needy, and blessing those who have less should be common practice. When housing or financially supporting someone for a significant amount of time, we must seek God to find out what He wants us to do. He is omniscient, omnipresent, and omnipotent. He is infinite, outside of time. He is everywhere at all times and at the same time.

I felt bad about the situation, but after praying and getting confirmation from many friends, I knew she needed to go. I told her she had a week. I explained that God had something else in mind for her and that it would not come unless I let her go. After a few days and another discussion, she knew I was not going to change my mind. She left.

Thank God for true friends. And praise the Lord for teaching me what a true friend is. My mom was instrumental in teaching me about friendship. There is no doubt in my mind that she prayed for me to receive this wisdom. In childhood and even in my early adulthood, I just couldn't pick 'em.

Due to a divine restriction, I was forced to spend time alone with God. Soon my mom's prayer was answered. The

Correction From a Brotha'

Lord started teaching me about relationships. The Word gave me wisdom about safe and unsafe people. In His time, when I was ready, people came into my life. Listening to the Holy Spirit and following His instruction gave me the ability to discern who was for me.

I have many friends, some believers and some not, who are happy for me when they are in a pit of despair and in my pit of despair when they are happy. We are walking our lives out together. We support each other through thick and thin and love each other. In addition, they are bold enough to tell me the truth in love.

Truth is something we need even when we don't want it. Warnings and correction are there to help us have an abundant life. It's enough that we have to deal with the enemy. So the Lord graciously put people in our lives to speak to us. He will use them to give us encouragement, love, truth, warning, and correction. True friends interrupt a budding romance or reveal a red flag regarding a decision we are about to make. They are a blessing. They offer wisdom and will be there to love us, whether the outcome of our choices is positive or negative.

Josh took a risk that day. This happened very early in our friendship. That day he told me the truth, even though it could have meant I would never speak to him again or would create a distance between us. Praise the Lord! Josh, John, and their wives are still friends of mine today, almost twenty years later.

However, was Josh the one who spoke those words? I'd asked God for a sign. Is it possible that Josh was overcome by the Holy Spirit and spoke under His unction? Or did

Chasing Fire

God allow Josh to be my friend at the precise moment I needed because, being the Maker of Josh, He foreknew how Josh would respond? Either way, it was God! He brought the sign and message I asked for.

The Word is filled with examples of God answering prayers and bringing signs through people. If he can use a donkey to speak on His behalf (Numbers 22:30), why not a person? Most people are familiar with the prophets Isaiah, Ezekiel, and Daniel, through whom the Lord spoke to leaders of nations. But I want to share some experiences of some prophets who don't have a book named after them. These are people you may not be very familiar with or heard of at all.

In Luke 2:25-35, we read about a man named Simeon. The Lord promised Simeon that he would see the Messiah before he passed away. The day that Jesus was going to be circumcised, eight days after his birth, Simeon was moved by the Holy Spirit to go to the Temple. When he saw Jesus, he had supernatural knowledge that the Babe was the Messiah. He lifted his voice, acknowledging that the promise of the Lord had been fulfilled and that Jesus was salvation.

> *Lord, now lettest thou thy servant depart in peace, according to thy word: For mine eyes have seen thy salvation, which thou hast prepared before the face of all people; a light to lighten the Gentiles, and the glory of thy people Israel* (Luke 2:29-32, KJV).

Correction From a Brotha'

In verses 36-38 of the same chapter, the prophetess Anna came into the Temple. She immediately gave thanks to the Lord and prophesied that the Babe was the redemption of Jerusalem.

In Acts 9, we read about Saul, a Jewish leader. Like many religious leaders of that day, Saul hated Christ and all who followed Him. Saul made it his mission to threaten the Christians and execute them for their beliefs. On his way to Damascus, the Lord Himself knocked Saul off his horse and asked him, "Why are you persecuting Me?" (verse 4).

Jesus told him to go to the city and wait. Blinded, he obeyed. Enter Ananias, a disciple in Damascus, whom the Lord visited in a vision. The Lord told him to go to Straight Street, lay hands on Saul, and heal his blindness. After hearing that Saul was God's chosen vessel, Ananias went to Saul and healed his blindness according to what the Lord had said. Later, Saul (or Paul) became the author of much of the New Testament under the inspiration of the Holy Spirit.

Simeon, Anna, and Ananias were three ordinary people of their day. They were not priests. They were not in paid, full-time ministry positions. The only thing they had was a right standing relationship with the Lord God. And that is all you need to be used by Him to bring blessing to others. Sometimes the Lord will use a stranger to speak to us, and sometimes He uses someone we know. For example, Moses' father-in-law, Jethro, advised Moses on how to handle disputes among all the people:

Chasing Fire

Now when Moses' father-in-law saw all that he was doing for the people, he said, "What is this thing that you are doing for the people? Why do you alone sit as judge and all the people stand about you from morning until evening? … The thing that you are doing is not good. You will surely wear out, both yourself and these people who are with you, for the task is too heavy for you; you cannot do it alone.

"Now listen to me: I will give you counsel, and God be with you. You be the people's representative before God, and you bring the disputes to God, then teach them the statutes and the laws, and make known to them the way in which they are to walk and the work they are to do.

"Furthermore, you shall select out of all the people able men who fear God, men of truth, those who hate dishonest gain; and you shall place these over them, as leaders of thousands, of hundreds, of fifties and of tens. Let them judge the people at all times; and let it be that every major dispute they will bring to you, but every minor dispute they themselves will judge. So it will be easier for you, and they will bear the burden with you.

"If you do this thing and God so commands you, then you will be able to endure, and all these people also will go to their place in peace." So Moses listened to his father-in-law and did all that he had said" (Exodus 18:14, 17-24 NASB).

Like my friend Josh, Jethro brought wisdom. It could have been a move of the Holy Spirit at that moment. Or perhaps God put Jethro in Moses' life, knowing his advice

Correction From a Brotha'

would be based on wisdom He had given throughout Jethro's life. Either way, it was God.

Earlier in the chapter, I shared my experience at a seminar. If God is extra-dimensional, infinite, all-powerful, all-knowing, at all places all the time, and residing outside of time, how could any finite person know whom He will speak to or how? God loves us and everybody gets to play in His game. He has no benchwarmers, subs, or second string. He has a position for each of us to play, and it's designed for our unique physical appearance, personality, strengths, and weaknesses. Therefore, we must not allow our flesh to tell us which one can hear from the Lord or which one the Lord will use for His glory. Everyone on the court needs to hear Him in order to know what to do or say next. Sometimes God will give these directions through family members, friends, or church leaders.

God has used many of his servants to keep me on the right path. Cheryl is my best friend. She called me one day, asking about this book and gave me a strong warning about my habit of procrastination. I thanked her for her prayers and for pushing me toward God's purposes in my life for the benefit of the Kingdom. God once used Rick, a member of my church, to give me a temporary job in his company and the use of his vehicle. Without these, I would not have been able to obey the Lord's call to India. Not only does God use believers and people in our life to correct us, but also to confirm and encourage the calling He has placed in us.

While I write this, we are getting ready to celebrate Thanksgiving. Many of my friends and family members

Chasing Fire

have written Facebook posts describing something they are thankful for. This is my post:

> Thank You, Lord, for bringing people into my life who love me enough to encourage and correct me. You have blessed me with them. I am extremely appreciative and do not take them, these true gifts from You, for granted. Thank You, Lord!

Six

A Sign To Encourage Us

Time was ticking. My buzzer had sounded, and certain promises from the Lord had not been delivered. He was more than late. There was no light at the end of the tunnel because there was no tunnel to begin with.

I had been walking with the Lord for seven years. Suddenly I felt lost and abandoned. Doubt rose in my heart, pushing a pointing, blaming finger at the Owner of everything. Like Allan Nolan in the film Bruce Almighty, I started complaining. "Hello! Are You there? You made all these promises. Where are they?"

When I finished ranting, raving, and throwing a spiritual temper tantrum, I collapsed on the couch, buried my face in my hands, and cried out to the Lord. "Why am I here? Where am I going? Did I hear You right? I need a sign, Lord. Please give me a sign so I'll know I'm in Your will and You are with me."

In my apartment, seeking His face and His will with a

Chasing Fire

pure heart, even though I was frustrated and at a loss, He heard me. I had asked for His help, and He gave me encouragement through a sign. The Holy Spirit came. With tears still in my eyes, He led me to my patio, which faced a huge northern Texas sky. There, right in front of me, was a beautiful rainbow accompanied by the best voice ever. "I'm here. Trust Me."

Many secular groups use the rainbow as a symbol. To me and millions of other believers in Christ throughout the world for centuries, the rainbow has been the sign of God's covenant promise, based on the historical record of Noah and the flood in the book of Genesis. It reminds us that God keeps His promises.

The sign was simple but personal. I specifically asked for a sign so I would know whether I was on the right track. My request was the result of doubting God's promise. God is so good. With a sign and four simple words, He dealt with my heart issue: a lack of trust.

I was wrecked. But God struck me with an overdose of His love. In one swift move, He proclaimed that His promises are yes and amen. He was with me and, though it was a difficult one, the path was right. I needed only to trust Him. The rainbow and the Lord's voice renewed me, encouraged me, and let me know I was on the right track with Him. I just had to be patient.

Our lives can be so complex, mysterious, and painfully challenging that we cry from our hearts to hear from heaven. We can't make decisions, can't see what's next and, at times, can't even go on. This causes us to need something greater than our own ability to fix it, make it right, or pick

A Sign To Encourage Us

the right path. Desperation leads to humility. When no one is around, when no one is looking, when no one is hearing, the words come. They may come through loud tears, an angry command, or a whisper, "God help me. Give me a sign. Just give me a sign."

I'd be willing to bet that most people have prayed that prayer at least once. We are not alone in looking for something supernatural to reveal the right way. When pressed, we look for answers outside our own wisdom when it has become fruitless. We come to the end of ourselves and pray.

Has an unseen event occurred in your life, such as an illness, death, unemployment, loss of possessions, or divorce? Are you a single mom or dad with responsibilities and expectations that you can no longer handle? Are you at a crossroads and have no idea which way to take? Be encouraged and reach for the great Encourager. He has an individualized prescription just for you.

The Lord loves to hear from us. A wonderful part of God's character allows us to come as we are. We can approach Him with raw emotions. Whether we are happy, content, mad, frustrated, afraid, sad, or silly, He accepts us as we are. We can be real. He knows how to realign our emotions in a way that does not bring judgment or guilt. This makes Him the safest Person for us to come to, raw and unfiltered. Nothing moves God faster than a prayer filled with raw, unfiltered truth.

In 1 Samuel, we read about Hannah, a barren woman needing a miracle. She needed God to breathe life into her womb so life could come forth. Her sorrow and anguish were so deep that her voice was silent. Only her lips moved.

As she prayed, her stature and demeanor caused the priest to believe she was drunk.

Desperation made her drop to her knees and make a vow to the only One who could hear her. If God gave her a son, she would give the son back to Him for life. The answer to her request came quickly.

Then Eli answered and said, "Go in peace; and may the God of Israel grant your petition that you have asked of Him." She said, "Let your maidservant find favor in your sight." So the woman went her way and ate, and her face was no longer sad. Then they arose early in the morning and worshiped before the Lord, and returned again to their house in Ramah. And Elkanah had relations with Hannah his wife, and the Lord remembered her. It came about in due time, after Hannah had conceived, that she gave birth to a son; and she named him Samuel, saying, "Because I have asked him of the Lord" (1 Samuel 1:17-20, NASB).

Another example of raw emotion displayed in heartfelt prayer was that of David. The Psalms are filled with his prayers of rejoicing, sorrow, discouragement, and praise. His prayers have inspired countless praise and worship songwriters and still do today. David often received his answer in the midst of his prayer. For example:

Help, Lord, for the godly man ceases to be, for the faithful disappear from among the sons of men. They

A Sign To Encourage Us

speak falsehood to one another; with flattering lips and with a double heart they speak. May the Lord cut off all flattering lips, the tongue that speaks great things; who have said, "With our tongue we will prevail; our lips are our own; who is lord over us?" "Because of the devastation of the afflicted, because of the groaning of the needy, now I will arise," says the Lord; "I will set him in the safety for which he longs." The words of the Lord are pure words, as silver tried in a furnace on the earth, refined seven times. Thou, O Lord, wilt keep them; Thou will preserve him from this generation forever. The wicked strut about on every side, when vileness is exalted among the sons of men (Psalm 12:1-8, NASB).

The heartfelt prayer is powerful. No wonder it is mentioned after God's directions for our spiritual armor in Ephesians 6:18. In addition, the heartfelt prayer will trump a selfish prayer. If prayers are like a hand of playing cards, the heartfelt prayer to be a bondservant to Christ (naming Him Lord over you) is the wildcard. It will trump all the others. As soon as the Lord hears this cry from His sheep, this verse becomes activated:

"For I know the plans that I have for you," declares the Lord, "plans for welfare and not for calamity to give you a future and a hope" (Jeremiah 29:11, NASB).

In my relationship with the Lord, I had submitted some strong, heartfelt prayers. I was consumed with God and His Word. I could not get enough. My time was filled with

Chasing Fire

Bible studies, serving in the church, and prayer meetings at my house. I used my vacation time to attend worship conferences, Christian concerts, and retreats. The only company I kept was with people who were on fire for the Lord—Jesus freaks. Whenever a scripture touched my spirit, I prayed it over my life. I had many high trumps and wildcards in my hands:

"Lord, use me for Your glory."

"Mold me in Your likeness."

"More of You, less of me, Lord."

"Purify my heart. Make me as gold and precious silver."

"Let me be in Your will, Lord. Don't let me miss it." (This is a major wildcard.)

This was how my prayer life was going until I started comparing myself to others. I looked at their circumstances, and my heart became consumed with wanting what they had, particularly marriage. Before I knew it, finding a life partner was something I thought about a lot. So much so, I started asking the Lord to "send me my husband."

The problem was that this prayer (though prayed many, many times) seemed to be fruitless. Time was flying by. Years passed and I was still single with no prospects.

Praying the Word proved powerful for me, so I started finding verses to pray so I would get what I wanted. The following seemed to fit the request:

Delight yourself also in the Lord, and He shall give you the desires of your heart (Psalm 37:4, NKJV).

A Sign To Encourage Us

The problem is that I used the verse improperly. First, I attempted to manipulate God with His Word in order to force Him to give me what I wanted. Then I took the verse out of context. I left out the verse before and after my verse. The entire text of Psalm 37:3-5 reads as follows:

Trust in the Lord, and do good; dwell in the land, and feed on His faithfulness. Delight yourself also in the Lord, and He shall give you the desires of your heart. Commit your way to the Lord, trust also in Him, and He shall bring it to pass (Psalm 37:3-5, NKJV).

After doing a word study on these verses, I found the Hebrew means this:

Verse 3: Put your hope and confidence in the Lord, do good, settle in the circumstance He has put you in and keep His steadfastness.

Verse 4: Live softly and delicately in the Lord. Then He will grant you the petitions of your inner man.

Verse 5: Roll away your way and put your hope and confidence in the Lord, and He will cause it to be.

The Bible teaches that our God is a jealous God (Exodus 20:5, Exodus 34:14, Deuteronomy 4:24, Deuteronomy 5:9, Deuteronomy 6:15, Joshua 24:19, Ezekiel 39:25, and Nahum 1:2.) If any passion, will, or desire is greater than our passion and desire for Him, we can end up making decisions that may seem right and good but are not God's will.

Chasing Fire

Think about the times you desperately wanted something, got it, and then discovered you really didn't want it at all. Psalm 37:3-5 is the guide to keep us from grasping things we think we want but really don't. God knows our hearts better than we do. He wants us to have His best.

Following the instructions of Psalm 37:3-5 will give power to our prayers because they are in agreement with God. It's similar to being in a staff meeting with a boss and giving an idea that rings true to the vision of the company and will cause success. The boss says, "You know, I was thinking the same thing. Let's do it!"

Prayer creates an atmosphere that allows the Lord to come and reside with us. It is more than sending requests and petitions for wants and needs. It builds our relationship and increases intimacy with Him. This two-way dialogue can be initiated by us or Him. If He calls first, listen and respond, then listen and respond some more. If we call to Him first, allow Him to respond. Give Him the opportunity to answer.

Have you ever had a friend who never let you get a word in edgewise? That is how we treat the Lord on most occasions. We get in a pickle or want something. When we are finished with our request, we say, "Amen," and then we move on to the next thing. God wants to respond to our prayers and for us to hear those answers, even when He says "no" or "wait."

Through prayer, we have the ability to influence the lives of others. We ask for a loved one's healing if they are ill. We ask for strength for a friend when they are discouraged. We ask for protections and wisdom for our leaders.

A Sign To Encourage Us

We ask that our children be kept safe. We ask the Lord to bring peace in chaos. These prayers are heard and answered.

The scriptures are filled with examples of prayer and the result of it. In Acts 12, while Peter was in prison due to his faith in Christ, the saints in the city prayed continually for his release. One night an angel of the Lord appeared before Peter and loosened his chains. Then he miraculously escorted Peter past two guard posts and out of the prison without being seen. Once they got past the prison gate and down the street, the angel disappeared.

Another example is found in Luke chapter one. Zacharias prayed that his barren wife would have a son. In the temple, the Lord told Zacharias that He'd heard his prayer. Later his wife, Elizabeth, became pregnant and bore a son, John the Baptist. A phrase repeated throughout the Old Testament is, "cried out to the Lord." It is followed by, "and He heard."

When we cried out to the Lord, He heard our voice and sent the Angel and brought us up out of Egypt (Numbers 20:16a, NKJV).

Then we cried out to the Lord God of our fathers, and the Lord heard our voice and looked on our affliction and our labor and our oppression (Deuteronomy 26:7, NKJV).

And he said, "I cried out to the Lord because of my affliction, and He answered me. Out of the belly of Sheol I cried, and You heard my voice" (Jonah 2:2, NKJV).

Chasing Fire

There is nothing like a baby's cry or scream. It is loud and continuous until the problem is rectified. Many use this as an example to reveal our natural sin and selfishness. I disagree with that example. Babies don't scream because they are selfish. Usually, they do it to get the adult to understand they are hungry, sleepy, or wet. None of those are selfish needs. The screaming and crying is their last resort to get the caregiver to understand their need because all the nonverbal cues given beforehand were missed. Praise God! He doesn't miss anything.

He looks down and reaches out to us when we are in need, in error, or in pain. He says, "What's wrong?" "Why are you sad?" or "What are you doing?" There are many examples of this in scripture, but my favorite is Genesis 4. In it, Cain was jealous of his brother Abel's favor with God, and he killed him. In verses 6-7, God spoke to Cain and warned him about his anger:

So the Lord said to Cain, "Why are you angry? And why has your countenance fallen? If you do well, will you not be accepted? And if you do not do well, sin lies at the door. And its desire is for you, but you should rule over it" (Genesis 4:6-7, NKJV).

God hears the heart cry. He heard Hannah's sorrow and Cain's anger. He hears the cry of our hearts as well. When we cry out to the Lord out of need and lay before His throne our brokenness, disappointment, pain, challenges, frustrations, confusion, and fears, He hears and moves on our behalf. We can come to Him about anything in our

A Sign To Encourage Us

lives or the lives of others. And we can continue to cry out until we get the answer, just like the infant and like the widow described in one of Jesus' parables:

> *Then He spoke a parable to them, that men always ought to pray and not lose heart, saying: "There was in a certain city a judge who did not fear God nor regard man. Now there was a certain widow in that city; and she came to him, saying, 'Get justice for me from my adversary.' And he would not for a while; but afterward he said within himself, 'Though I do not fear God nor regard man, yet because this widow troubles me I will avenge her, lest by her continual coming she weary me.' Then the Lord said, "Hear what the unjust judge said. And shall God not avenge His own elect who cry out day and night to Him, though He bears long with them? I tell you that He will avenge them speedily"* (Luke 18:1-8a, NKJV).

This reminds me of the continued cry my family made for the health of my cousin Amiya. She was born with a rare brain defect that would require many risky surgeries and could result in things no one likes to hear or think about. Her first major surgery was when she was one month old. My family remained before the throne of God, begging for His intervention. Years later and after five surgeries, she is now completely healthy.

Life can get us down. It's nice to know that the Creator cares for each of us. He understands our afflictions and sufferings. He knows we get discouraged and feel hopeless. He

Chasing Fire

also knows exactly what sign will strengthen us to continue on. Jesus commands,

> *Come to Me, all you who labor and are heavy laden, and I will give you rest* (Matthew 11:28, NKJV).

When translated from the Greek, the verse calls for those burdened with grief, exhaustion, or weariness to come to Him, and He will cease the burden to give strength needed to deal with whatever circumstance is weighing us down. He may do that through a sign.

God often used signs throughout Scripture. In Exodus, He used the plagues as signs to the Egyptians to release the Israelites from captivity. In the books of the prophets, He used signs to warn, correct, and bless His people (Jonah 1-2; Ezekiel 5). In Matthew 24, Jesus lists many signs of His second coming and the end of days. He uses them to build our faith and restore hope.

The rainbow restored my hope and added strength to His blind fold called faith. I take one step at a time as He directs. It reminds me of being in a limousine with the partition up. You don't have to worry about the signs, signals, traffic, or how to get where you're going. You are with close friends, headed to a great destination, enjoying the ride, and trusting that before long the driver will announce your arrival. If discouragement comes again or a pause in the process seems long, knock on the partition, knowing your Driver will give you the information you need in order to continue with faith and patience. That information may come through the Word, His voice, or a sign.

Seven

Spirit Inspired

One day, winter came to my door in the form of icy rain. I didn't know that I was soon to be drenched in ice water of another kind.

I couldn't believe it. According to two witnesses on two separate occasions, people I thought were my friends and believers had been backbiting and gossiping about me.

This was my first experience of being hurt by Christians. Feelings of betrayal, sadness, and anger flooded me. Then fear overcame me because they were well-known, God-fearing people. What if I would lose other friends because of this? I had already become accustomed to Romans 12:19 (NASB): "Vengeance is Mine, I will repay, says the Lord."

Taking revenge was out of God's will for me. At that moment, I didn't like this verse very much. My mind was filled with how I could defend myself and get justice.

Frustrated and hurt, I came to the Lord. The Word says

Chasing Fire

come as you are, so I came before Him confused, frustrated, hurt, and mad! Ranting and raving soon turned to tears. I was at my wits' end. My thoughts were consumed with this circumstance.

I often use poetry as an outlet for expressing my feelings. So I sat down and wrote a poem. This poem is unlike any other I have ever written. The experience is etched in the memory of my spirit.

A Cry's Answer

Lord God, my Savior! Hold me tightly in Your arms.
There are tongues of slander meaning to scar.
As buzzards do flesh, the words eat at my spirit.
And though they don't know, my ears are hearing it.

Oh, my soul, Lord Jesus, please mend
Many of these words from the lips of friends.
Tears flow like rain. I want to run and hide
Although Your Word says You are by my side.

I crawl to the cross. Make my armor new
And teach me, Lord. What should I do?

This first part of the poem is normal. Anyone who enjoys poetry can accept it. But the second part is peculiar. Why? Because I didn't write it out of myself as I did the first part. The first verse was for me. I had no intention of writing a second verse.

Spirit Inspired

I put down the pen. Then out of nowhere, I picked it up again and resumed writing. This is what followed:

My sweet, sweet child. You need not be afraid.
For things such as this, the price has been paid.
Do not fret or fear wounds of slander and rejection.
I will use this to mold you, closer to my perfection.

Be filled with compassion; walk as I did.
And be cautious now, with the words from your lips.
These earthly circumstances may not seem fair today
But keep hope and the faith. I am on my way.

For there will come a time when all will give account,
For every word chosen to come from the mouth.
And when I return, I will make it all right.
Let Me lift your head, shine through you with light.

Do not retaliate. And do not curse.
My instruction to you is to do the reverse.
Bless persecutors, enemy, or friend.
And see my glory, the power that mends.

Have mercy, serve, give grace as above.
But most important, I command you to love.

I can't explain this. I was writing with my hand, but it was not me. The Holy Spirit took control and brought my answer through my own hand.

Chasing Fire

When I put down the pen the second time and read what was written, I was encouraged! I hung onto the first four words, "My sweet, sweet child," for awhile. My tears were transformed into medicine, and a smile came to my face. God accepts me. God loves me and I am His.

He could have stopped there, but He didn't because in addition to the first phrase, we all need to know the rest of what He said. God loves and calls us His very own. Jesus paid it all. That crimson flow covers our sins and the sins of those who afflict us. He sees our afflictions in this fallen world and will make things right. We have to trust Him and allow the identity of Christ to manifest through us, even though people, events, and circumstances sometimes bring pain, sorrow, frustration, anger, etc. In the midst of all that is ugly, we are commanded to love.

Did you notice He didn't mention how or when He intended to get those people back? Think of it this way. I have two little sisters. Whenever any of us did something to hurt the other, we had a consequence. The level of the consequence fit the level of the crime. My parents came to the defense of the injured sibling and brought justice. We did not bring the justice. In addition, the consequence was given in private.

One of the problems with the church is that real people are there. They are all imperfect and have mouths. Mouths + Sin + Flesh = Hurting Someone Else's Feelings. I have been on both sides of that equation. We know that being on the right side of the equation is not fun. But let's be honest. Being on the left side isn't fun either, especially when you're confronted about it.

Spirit Inspired

Many times, more than I can count, I have been on the right side. Slander, backbiting, and rejection have been the order of not a day but many seasons throughout my life. Almost every year, winter comes for me. It is cold, dark, and isolating; and it feels as if a blizzard is blocking my vision. Freezing words burn my soul and attempt to inflict frostbite on my heart.

Though many winters have come and gone, my heart and soul are not callused. Therefore, at the knock of bitter coldness, the pain is freshly anew. Inquiries to the Lord and pleas for winterless life still continue.

But God is good. He pulls me through every time. Winter ends and spring comes. I am renewed and refreshed by His still waters where He restores my soul. Then he prepares a table for me before my enemies, and goodness continues to follow me because I dwell in the house of the Lord (Psalms 23.)

At times, I wonder if this is a result of my own sin or something I am reaping due to what I have sown. Is this a Job-like situation, in which the devil and the Lord have a bet? I don't know, and it doesn't matter. My recourse is to respond to these things in a Christ-like manner. The Holy Spirit pulls me through it and heals me so I always become better and not bitter.

As believers, we all live in God's house. When we hurt one another, He deals with us. He is not mean or abusive, but He does lovingly correct. As one who has been chastised before, I knew that my spiritual siblings were about to have a supernatural visit. God would take care of it. I did not know how. But the poem allowed me to put it in His hands and trust that He would mend my heart as I blessed and loved them anyway.

The only other place I have seen something like my poem is in the Psalms penned by King David. Yes, David was a king and I'm not. David was a gifted musician and singer. I'm not. David was an awesome warrior. I am not. The only thing we have in common is the love of the Lord. I cannot explain the creation of this poem. My hands wrote it, but at the same time, I cannot take credit for all of it.

Experiences are great, but they are from God only if they're backed by the Word. Supernatural experiences happen when we serve the God of the universe. However, the enemy of our souls will try to deceive us with counterfeit experiences spawned by himself and his dominion. God will not do anything against His own character, attributes, and inspired Word. All supernatural experiences should point to and/or intensify our relationship with God, Jesus, and the Holy Spirit. The litmus test for a supernatural experience is to see whether it points to Him, gives Him glory, and conforms to His character or word. Therefore, let's take a look at my poem in this light.

The poem is in two verses. The first verse I wrote out of pain and anger. I have already divulged that my flesh wanted to vindicate myself and take revenge, but I went to the Lord instead. It is safe to believe that we can all agree the first verse is acceptable. The words in the second verse are all scripturally sound. Every concept can be backed by the Word. Below each concept is supported by at least one corresponding verse from the Bible:

Spirit Inspired

Scriptural References for Poem

My sweet, sweet child.

I am the good shepherd; and I know my sheep, and am known by My own (John 10:14, NKJV).

Know that the Lord, He is God; It is He who has made us, and not we ourselves; we are His people and the sheep of His pasture (Psalm 100:3, NKJV).

The Spirit Himself bears witness with our spirit that we are children of God (Romans 8:16, NKJV).

You need not be afraid.

For God has not given us a spirit of fear, but of power and of love and of a sound mind (2 Timothy 1:7, NKJV).

So, we may boldly say: "The Lord is my helper; I will not fear. What can man do to me?" (Hebrews 13:6, NKJV).

For things such as this, the price has been paid.

Therefore take heed to yourselves and to all the flock, among which the Holy Spirit has made you overseers, to shepherd the church of God which He purchased with His own blood (Acts 20:28, NKJV).

Do not fret or fear wounds of slander and rejection.

I will use this to mold you, closer to my perfection.

Chasing Fire

My brethren, count it all joy when you fall into various trials, knowing that the testing of your faith produces patience (James 1:2-3, NKJV).

But even if you should suffer for righteousness' sake, you are blessed. "And do not be afraid of their threats, nor be troubled" (1 Peter 3:14, NKJV).

Be filled with compassion; walk as I did.

Finally, all of you be of one mind, having compassion for one another; love as brothers, be tenderhearted, be courteous (1 Peter 3:8, NKJV).

For this is commendable, if because of conscience toward God one endures grief, suffering wrongfully. For what credit is it if, when you are beaten for your faults, you take it patiently? But when you do good and suffer, if you take it patiently, this is commendable before God. For to this you were called, because Christ also suffered for us, leaving us an example, that you should follow His steps (1 Peter 2:19-21, NKJV).

And be cautious now, with words from your lips.

Set a guard, O Lord, over my mouth; keep watch over the door of my lips (Psalm 141:3, NKJV).

Keep your tongue from evil, and your lips from speaking deceit (Psalm 34:13, NKJV).

Spirit Inspired

These earthly circumstances may not seem fair today
But keep hope and the faith. I am on my way.

*Why are you cast down, O my soul? And why are you
disquieted within me? Hope in God, for I shall yet
praise Him for the help of His countenance* (Psalm
42:5, NKJV).

*For what is our hope, or joy, or crown of rejoicing? Is it
not even you in the presence of our Lord Jesus Christ at
His coming?* (1 Thessalonians 2:19, NKJV)

For there will come a time when all will give account,
For every word chosen to come from the mouth.

*They will give an account to Him who is ready to judge
the living and the dead* (1 Peter 4:5, NKJV).

*Indeed, let God be true but every man a liar. As it is
written: "That You may be justified in Your words, And
may overcome when You are judged"* (Romans 3:4,
NKJV).

And when I return, I will make all right.

*Behold, I am coming quickly! Blessed is he who keeps the
words of the prophecy of this book* (Revelation 22:7,
NKJV).

*And behold, I am coming quickly, and My reward is
with Me, to give to every one according to his work*
(Revelation 22:12, NKJV).

And I saw the dead, small and great, standing before God, and books were opened. And another book was opened, which is the Book of Life. And the dead were judged according to their works, by the things which were written in the books (Revelation 20:12, NKJV).

Let Me lift your head, shine through you with light.

But You, O Lord, are a shield for me, My glory and the One who lifts up my head (Psalm 3:3, NKJV).

And now my head shall be lifted up above my enemies all around me; therefore I will offer sacrifices of joy in His tabernacle; I will sing, yes, I will sing praises to the Lord (Psalm 27:6, NKJV).

Do not retaliate. And do not curse.
My instruction to you is to do the reverse.
Bless persecutors, enemy, or friend.
And see my glory, power that mends.

Bless those who persecute you; bless and do not curse (Romans 12:14, NKJV).

But I say to you, love your enemies, bless those who curse you, do good to those who hate you, and pray for those who spitefully use you and persecute you (Matthew 5:44, NKJV).

Finally, all of you be of one mind, having compassion for one another; love as brothers, be tenderhearted, be courteous; not returning evil for evil or reviling for re-

Spirit Inspired

viling, but on the contrary blessing, knowing that you were called to this, that you may inherit a blessing (1 Peter 3:8-9, NKJV).

Have mercy, serve; give grace as above.

For judgment is without mercy to the one who has shown no mercy. Mercy triumphs over judgment (James 2:13, NKJV).

Let your speech always be with grace, seasoned with salt, that you may know how you ought to answer each one (Colossians 4:6, NKJV).

But most important, I command you to love.

"Teacher, which is the great commandment in the law?" Jesus said to him, "'You shall love the Lord your God with all your heart, with all your soul, and with all your mind.' This is the first and great commandment. And the second is like it: 'You shall love your neighbor as yourself.' On these two commandments hang all the Law and the Prophets" (Matthew 22:36-40, NKJV).

We see that scripture supports the second verse of the poem. One question remains. Did the Holy Spirit come down, take control of my hand, and answer? Was this inspired by the Holy Spirit? Some people will say yes, and some will say no. The experiences we have with the Father through Christ and His Spirit may be received by others—or not. We should not let the opinions of others discourage us from continuing our journey with Him or cause us to leave the church. We should use wisdom when sharing our relationship to God with others. Remember they are pearls, precious moments between you and the Father.

God is a supernatural Being. Anything is possible with Him. He will do anything at anytime with anybody in any way He sees fit. He is Lord and He is sovereign. We are dust walking. In our prayers, we should ask the Lord to use us as a blessing, no matter what that looks like. We are instruments in His hands. This poem is what He decided to play that day through me, for me and for anyone who reads it. God loves us. He speaks to us and through us for our blessing and His glory.

My prayer is that this experience blesses you and sparks a desire for a relationship with God that will bring you into all sorts of awesome, supernatural experiences. Why not? He is an awesome, supernatural God!

Eight

Supernatural Living

Sitting in my backyard with a sign saying, "For Free," I watched all my possessions disappear in less than an hour. The Holy Spirit, as the wind for my sails, was taking me to another place. The Captain of my heart required that I put almost everything I owned in the hands of others who lacked the basic necessities of life. An unexpected street-wide yard sale gave me the opportunity to obey before leaving. Everything was gone. The following Monday, I packed my clothes in my vehicle, along with some personal items and $100 in cash, and headed to Austin, Texas, for the first time.

Once in an apartment, I had to cry out to the Lord because I had no furniture. No bed, couch, dishes—nothing. Work paid only the bills. Though I am very particular and like to have a color scheme that goes throughout the home, I was ready to receive anything. Standing in the middle of this small, empty place I said a quick prayer, "Lord, fill it!"

Chasing Fire

Within a month's time, my apartment was almost completely furnished. I didn't ask, but people felt it in their heart to give me things. They heard I had moved and asked if I wanted or needed anything. Bob Canfield, a true brother in Christ and friend, surprised me with a phone call. He told me that he knew a man in prison who was looking to give away all his possessions. Through this prisoner, I received a couch, love seat, chair, two end tables, and a coffee table. The tables even matched the cedar wall in my apartment.

Another call came from believers, offering the gift of a matching dish set, complete with plates, bowls, saucers, drinking glasses, teacups, and silverware. A different family from another church gave me pots and pans. The main color of the dish set and pots and pans was an exact match with my new couches.

Finally, a friend gave me a dining room table and chairs. This table went beautifully with the coffee and end tables and the cedar wall. Everything matched, although the donors didn't know each other. And my new things were way better than what I gave away. Was this a coincidence? No. God furnished my apartment based on my particular style. I needed the furniture, but the style was "just because."

Are you ready for some supernatural "just because" in your life? These experiences are in store for all of us. He has the plan, and He will provide everything we need to see it through. Therefore, it is crucial to hear God and stay attuned to His leading.

As a student of the Word of God, I came across a truth

that threads through the entire text. God is powerful. He can do whatever He wants with anyone or anything, at any time. This includes things that defy scientific truths, such as the burning bush that was not consumed (Exodus 3:2.) In my prayer time, I asked the Lord for personal experiences of His power and to be an eyewitness of His miracles. I prayed this way every day.

Praise God! I witnessed the power of the Holy Spirit in the mid-90s, during the Toronto Blessing through the Vineyard, a non-denominational church founded by John Wimber. During this outpouring, people were refreshed with a personal touch from heaven. Awesome things happened in the Lord. However, I wanted to see the sea split wide or be able to walk on water like Peter. My prayers continued. After many years of begging Him to let me experience or at least see a supernatural lifestyle in Him, He delivered.

While I was serving in missions to India, the Lord served me a platter of miracles. Angelic visitations, healings, dealing with demonic attack, and watching the church leaders behave, move, and testify of things in the same manner as the apostles in the Bible was like being in a blockbuster film. This, coupled with God's voice, was more than anything I could have asked for. I was high on Jesus and totally addicted. My trips to India were the answer to a long-time prayer. They tested me and taught me more about God. What I treasure most is the fine-tuning of my spiritual ears to hear His voice. Coming back to the United States I was addicted to God, His Word, His ways, and His voice. My experiences abroad taught me that God has a

Chasing Fire

special interest in each person's life. He loves every one—each person who was ever born and ever will be born.

For God so loved the world, that He gave His only begotten Son, that whoever believes in Him shall not perish, but have eternal life (John 3:16, NASB).

But God demonstrates His own love toward us, in that while we were yet sinners, Christ died for us (Romans 5:8, NASB).

The Lord is not slow about His promise, as some count slowness, but is patient toward you, not wishing for any to perish but for all to come to repentance (2 Peter 3:9, NASB).

Having a close relationship with the Creator affords immeasurable benefits. He grants peace and joy in the midst of chaos. He delivers keys to unlock questions regarding our role and purpose in the timeline of our existence.

With a word from heaven, He will fix a life that most would call a dream but the one living it calls a nightmare. This type of closeness with God means we must hear Him. Hearing supernatural answers to our questions about our life will bring the food that fills and satisfies the inner man. He speaks in many ways. Some of these ways are not bound to natural explanation but are supernatural.

Hearing God's voice and experiencing the supernatural are not deeply discussed in the church at large. However, our culture has embraced and become intrigued by the supernatural, such as déjà vu experiences, women's intuition, and having a sixth sense and premonitions. The supernatural is becoming more and more popular. This is evident through top-rated television programs and blockbuster films such as *The Medium, The Ghost Hunters, Grimm, Paranormal Activity, Harry Potter,* and the *Twilight* series.

These programs and films feature characters who are endowed with supernatural capabilities. These "gifts" allow them to see the unseen, know the unknown, move things with their mind, have dreams and visions of warning, or live forever without aging. The world has presented them as fantasy and science fiction, not real. Claims of experiencing such things are met with disbelief, silence, a change of subject, or humor.

I submit that they aren't fantasy or science fiction. They're real. The supernatural is reality. The Bible says that with God, all things are possible. Thereby, our impossible imaginations and dreams are possible with God.

And looking at them Jesus said to them, "With people this is impossible, but with God all things are possible" (Matthew 19:26, NASB).

In addition, many of the supernatural abilities displayed in these science fiction and fantasy films are in the Bible. For example, Samson is the real man of steel. The only thing he doesn't do is fly and leap over tall buildings. He was unable to be hurt or killed until his kryptonite was discovered by the Philistines, and they captured him. Endowed

Chasing Fire

with supernatural strength by the Spirit of the Lord he did the following:

- Tore a lion to pieces with his bare hands (Judges 14:6).
- Made ropes he was bound with melt like flax from fire from his skin (Judges 15:14).
- Slew a thousand men with the jaw bone of a donkey (Judges 15:15).
- Broke seven wet bowstrings he was bound with, using heat from his body (Judges 16:9).
- With his bare hands brought down a temple by knocking down the pillars that held it up (Judges 16:29-30).

John saw the future (the book of Revelation), Phillip ran and overtook a chariot (Acts 8:29-30) and then was transported (beamed up like on Star Trek) from one spot to another about twenty miles away (Acts 8:39-40), and Jesus and His followers performed more healings than we could list. Other supernatural occurrences in the Bible include the parting of the Red Sea, Peter walking on water, Jonah's survival in the stomach of a fish, Jesus' birth from a virgin, Jesus' resurrection, and Sarah and Abraham having a son way past menopause and seed production.

Furthermore, there are people today who display these abilities and others outlined in scripture. Let's take it a step further. We are supposed to be operating in at least one of them. While living on this earth, each of us has a purpose, a destiny etched in the eternal calendar of God's Kingdom. It's there, whether we know it and grasp it or not.

Supernatural Living

For the gifts and the calling of God are irrevocable. (Romans 11:29, NKJV).

This means they are not assigned to anyone else. Our gifts and callings may be similar, but each has a specific purpose for the person assigned. For example, one may be called to teach and have the gift of supernatural discernment because he/she will have a child in the class who is being abused. The natural talent, with career experience and accompanied by the spiritual gift, is what will bring that child to safety.

Or maybe someone is called to be an evangelist with the gift of healing in order to bring healing to someone else. This person then shares their testimony of healing to reach another sick person looking for hope.

There is a lot of dispute about spiritual gifts throughout the body of Christ. Some believers say they no longer function and aren't needed. Others say they are. Some believe it is not possible to hear God unless _____ (fill in the blank). Not true. Faith is in the list of gifts. If faith is for today, so is prophecy and healing. Here is a quick list of the gifts in the Bible with their corresponding verse. At least one of them is for you.

- Romans 12:6-8: Prophecy, teaching, ministry, exhortation, giving, leadership, mercy
- 1 Corinthians 12:4-11: Wisdom, knowledge, faith, healing, working of miracles, prophecy, discerning of spirits, differing tongues, interpretation of tongues

- 1 Corinthians 12:28: Apostles, prophets, teachers, miracles, gifts of healings, helps, administrations, varieties of tongues.

In the beginning of this book, I explained that a miracle is an inexplicable occurrence done by God, like raising the dead or walking on water. The documentary *Finger of God* cites miracles and testimonies of the miraculous. My favorite is a testimony of food multiplication. Heidi Baker is a missionary in Africa, called by God to feed and take care of children there. On one specific occasion, for example, food was delivered for their meal, but it was obvious that it wasn't enough for everyone. After they prayed over the food, they passed the tray around, and everyone received a good portion. The food multiplied as did the fish and loaves during Jesus' ministry. Heidi, along with her husband, their volunteers, and the help of God, feeds thousands of children a day.

God doesn't want us just to live. He wants us endowed with supernatural capabilities to serve Him, a supernatural God. Therefore, we must hear Him to know what our power is and how He wants us to use it. There are some hindrances to receiving all of His promises. First, we must be comfortable with how He made us. We must accept who we are and everything about us in order to be all we can be. Unfortunately, we often conform to social pressures to be what others want us to be. As a result, we use masks, putting on whichever fits for the people we are around or the situation in which we find ourselves.

Moreover, some of us have overprescribed ourselves

Supernatural Living

with self-help books, television shows, seminars, conferences, and classes. Our bodies, minds, personality, vocal tones, facial expressions, and body language are placed on a table before a plethora of chisels. Each chisel is in the hand of someone who wants personal growth according to their philosophy and not the truth of God's Word. Before too long, things are chiseled away that God intended to stay or things added that He had no intention for us to have.

It is amazing how many people with chisels have come into my life. I have had people wonder why I wear heels when I'm six feet tall. Some have told me to change my presence or energy level, to be silent or to speak up, to do this or do that.

I am guilty of the same. Growing and getting better are good if we change according to what the Lord—not the world—has in store. But most of the time, our chisels shape us according to the expectations of others or according to what we want or find comfortable.

We need to put down our chisels. Instead, look up to the Perfect Chiseler in prayer and ask Him to mold us and others to into what He needs, no matter what that looks like to us. The idea that God would allow the expectations of men to dictate His plan is ridiculous. It places the destiny of people into the hands of fallible men instead of the hands of an omnipotent, omniscient, omnipresent, holy, and perfect God.

But now, O Lord, you are our Father; we are the clay, and You our potter and all we are the work of Your hand (Isaiah 64:8 NKJV).

Another hindrance is how we respond to mistakes—both our own and those of others. We bog ourselves down with regrets. Our mind is plagued with thoughts of unworthiness. As imperfect humans, we make unwise choices and decisions that can cause consequences no one wants. The blessing is that God already knows our mistakes and those we are yet to commit. He has planned accordingly, due to His omniscience. Like children bring their broken toys to their dads to fix, we must get in the habit of bringing all our broken things to our Father in heaven, who is eager to make it all right.

Bless the Lord, O my soul, and forget not all His benefits; who forgives all your iniquities, who heals all your diseases, who redeems your life from destruction, who crowns you with lovingkindness and tender mercies, who satisfies your mouth with good things, so that your youth is renewed like eagle's (Psalm 103:2-5, NKJV).

As far as the east is from the west, so far has He removed our transgressions from us (Psalm 103:12, NKJV).

There is therefore now no condemnation to those who are in Christ Jesus, who do not walk according to the flesh, but according to the Spirit. For the law of the Spirit of life in Christ Jesus has made me free from the law of sin and death (Romans 8:1-2, NKJV).

Come to Me, all you who labor and are heavy laden, and I will give you rest (Matthew 11:28, NKJV).

Supernatural Living

Finally, some of us are hindered by our birth circumstances or the family into which we were born. We make mistakes but God does not create mistakes. God will allow and use our wrong decisions for His glory and work it out for our benefit (Romans 8:28). In other words, if you were born out of wedlock, given up for adoption, born to irresponsible parents, it doesn't matter. You still have an individualized plan and call on your life. We are told in the Psalms that the Lord knit each of us in the womb. We have looked at this verse before, but let's look at it again.

For You formed my inward parts; You covered me in my mother's womb. I will praise You, for I am fearfully and wonderfully made; marvelous are Your works, and that my soul knows very well. My frame was not hidden from You, when I was made in secret, and skillfully wrought in the lowest parts of the earth. Your eyes saw my substance, being yet unformed. And in Your book they all were written, the days fashioned for me, when as yet there were none of them. How precious also are Your thoughts to me, O God! How great is the sum of them! If I should count them, they would be more in number than the sand; when I awake, I am still with You (Psalm 139:13-18, NKJV).

Awesome! The days fashioned for each one of us are already written down. His thoughts toward us are innumerable. The love of God for us is so great, we can't fathom it. It is impossible to understand the heartbeat He has for each of us. He knows life here is hard and challenging. We aren't

Chasing Fire

perfect but He chooses to bless us anyway. King David is a perfect example of this. He is described as having a heart after God, a great King who loved the Lord with his whole being.

> *And when He had removed him, He raised up for them David as king, to whom also He gave testimony and said, "I have found David the Son of Jesse, a man after my own heart, who will do all My will"* (Acts 13:22, NKJV).

Well, King David had some drama in his life. He had an affair with the wife of one of his most loyal subjects. Then he killed his loyal subject to cover up the sin. Even though King David was called to repent for his actions many times, he fulfilled His destiny because of his relationship with God. Through the ups and downs of the King's life, he lived successfully. He hit the mark and endured with love, peace, and joy. The historical record of King David is found in 1 Samuel 16 through 1 Kings 2.

To have a life with love, peace, and joy even in times of pain, trial and suffering, to have a life work that makes your heart glad even on difficult days, and to have an unexplainable, supernatural ability to prosper in everything your hand touches, you need one thing: an ear to hear.

> *But his delight is in the law of the Lord, and in His law he meditates day and night. He shall be like a tree planted by the rivers of water, that brings forth its fruit*

Supernatural Living

in its season, whose leaf also shall not wither; and whatever he does shall prosper (Psalm 1:2-3, NKJV).

Then you shall call, and the Lord will answer; you shall cry, and He will say, "Here I am." If you take away the yoke from your midst, the pointing of the finger, and speaking wickedness, if you extend your soul to the hungry and satisfy the afflicted soul, then your light shall dawn in the darkness, and your darkness shall be as the noonday. The Lord will guide you continually, and satisfy your soul in drought, and strengthen your bones; you shall be like a watered garden, and like a spring of water, whose waters do not fail (Isaiah 58:9-11, NKJV).

Perfect attendance in church cannot do it. Religiosity and tradition cannot do it. A marriage cannot do it. A new marriage cannot do it. Having children cannot do it. Nothing on this earth can do it in and of itself. These things morph, transform, and change over time. They are not solid, unbreakable truths that can take you through anything this world puts in your face, from victory to defeat, agony to pleasure, or success to failure. We all need an ear to hear.

Hearing and listening to God results in a life of love, peace, and joy. These three things (love, peace, and joy) are the fruit of the Spirit that bears witness to God's existence in a person's life.

*But the fruit of the Spirit is love, joy, peace, longsuf-
fering, kindness, goodness, faithfulness, gentleness, self-
control. Against such there is no law. And those who are
Christ's have crucified the flesh with its passions and desires. If we live in the Spirit, let us also walk in the
Spirit* (Galatians 5:22-25, NKJV).

These wings carry people through the worst of disasters
and calamities, despair and depression that the world can
hand over. The dust falls and the Spirit carries us up
through the ashes, through the rain, through a dark night
to a new dawn. Operating as a force field, bitterness and
hopelessness do not stand a chance.

But that's not all. There is much more, including a direct connection to the Creator of the universe. He has the
plan, and He wants to tell you about it. The idea of God
speaking to us is the key to hearing and knowing every
wonderful, awesome thing He has for us. "Onward,
Christian Soldiers" is not just for a reward in the afterlife. It
is for blessings in the here and now. I can write this only
because I have experienced it myself and am desperate for
every person to know this truth:

*So Jesus said to them, "Assuredly I say to you, that in the
regeneration, when the Son of Man sits on the throne of
His glory, you who have followed Me will also sit on
twelve thrones, judging the twelve tribes of Israel. And
everyone who has left houses or brothers or sisters or father or mother or wife or children or lands for my name's
sake, shall receive a hundredfold, and inherit eternal
life"* (Matthew 19:28-29, NKJV).

In the above passage, Jesus was encouraging the twelve disciples with what their reward would be in heaven. They will sit on thrones and judge the tribes of Israel in the millennial Kingdom spoken of in the book of Revelation. But everybody will get a hundredfold of whatever they leave to obey God while on earth—plus eternal life.

God loves you. He is the perfect Father. He cares about you individually. He even cares about the small things no one else would think or know about, "just because" of His love for you.

He wants us to hear Him, know His plan, and receive the supernatural gifts we will need for our journey and destiny. The Lord will speak to us in many wondrous ways. We may hear His voice, feel a nudging in our gut, or have a dream or vision. He may use a person or group of people to speak a word of prophecy, encouragement, or correction. He may use the manifestation of His presence or His word. But whatever way He chooses, it will be just what you need.

Throughout the rest of this book, we will look at some of these supernatural powers. We will gain knowledge of their existence and use in biblical times and read about the supernatural experiences of people living today.

Nine

Seeing the Unseen

TESTIMONY

Many years ago, I came into work one day and received some unfortunate news. My friend's wife, Sheila, had died. After hearing what happened, my mind was focused on thoughts of her and her husband, especially their walk with the Lord. I began to pray for the family.

While stocking shelves, I had an open vision. Within the boxes of food, a window opened. It held my friend Sheila's face. She said, "Go get 'em, Gina!" And that was it. The window closed and the boxes on the shelves in front of me re-appeared.

I had not been to a funeral before, but I knew my experience would be encouraging. The vision revealed to my spirit that Sheila was before the Lord. I first shared it with my pastor and then with Sheila's sister. They were blessed by it, and the family was encouraged. Confirmation of the vision did not come until six months later.

While flying home from my Bible college, I was reading a book about heaven. In it, the author described a stadium of believers looking down to those still remaining on earth, cheering them on with the words, "Go get 'em!" This was encouraging to me, because it let me know that the vision I had of Sheila months earlier was from the Lord.

—*Gina Prince, Stay-at-Home Mom*

My husband and I have enjoyed participating on prophetic evangelism teams for outreaches at different venues, such as the Sundance Film Festival. The purpose of the outreach is to minister to people with words of encouragement, wisdom, knowledge, prophecy, and dream interpretation. During a season of learning, we served at Venice Beach, under the leadership of Doug Addison, founder of InLight Connection and author of *No More Christianese*.

While talking with a young man at one of these outreaches, I had a vision. A conversation that began with the beauty of the day turned to things not so beautiful. The young man began to share a heartbreaking story with me.

Suddenly in the middle of his story, I saw a picture over his head: he was painting on a canvas. Knowledge came to my mind as I saw him painting.

When he was finished talking, I said, "Dude. You are an awesome painter. Why did you give it up?"

Since nothing in his story related to any form of art, he

responded to me with a stony stare and asked, "Who are you? How did you know I paint?"

I shared that the Lord had revealed his gift of art to me. Furthermore, I told him that his talent in art was important to the Lord because He wanted to bless him in that area of his life.

Tears came to his eyes as the whole group gave him words of encouragement to continue in his God-given talent. He received the encouragement and asked us to pray for him on the spot. After the prayer, the young man who came to us brokenhearted left us encouraged and with his countenance lifted.

In the previous chapter, we mentioned movies and television programs with characters who display supernatural abilities. Hollywood has portrayed many characters with the gift of sight. For example, in the film *Push*, one of the characters could see the future and predict what was going to happen, based on pictures she saw and drew. In the film *Men in Black 3* was a character who could see different outcomes of the future, based on the responses and choices people made.

But Hollywood has nothing on the God of the universe. These fictitious stories display supernatural abilities, but God was moving through people supernaturally long before the art of dramatization and film. Seeing the unseen is one of many supernatural experiences. It is a real thing that can happen to any of us as a way for God to send a message from heaven.

And it shall come to pass afterward that I will pour out My Spirit on all flesh; your sons and your daughters shall prophesy, your old men shall dream dreams, your young men shall see visions. And also on My menservants and on My maidservants I will pour out My spirit in those days (Joel 2:28-29, NKJV).

The word "seer" is used twenty-two times in twenty verses of the NKJV and the NASB Bible translations. The word "seers" is used four times in four verses in the same translations. Though nine men are named as seers, scripture implies by using the plural form of the word that there were many more than the nine named. In the table below, you will find the nine seers named and the scripture references for them. Other seers in scripture are Isaiah, Ezekiel, and Daniel. Their visions are recorded in the books named after them. Another is Stephen who, after bringing a strong message of correction to the religious leaders, saw a vision while being stoned to death:

But he, being full of the Holy Spirit, gazed into heaven and saw the glory of God, and Jesus standing at the right hand of God, and said, "Look! I see the heavens opened and the Son of Man standing at the right hand of God!" (Acts 7:55-56, NKJV)

On the next page is a chart that lists some of the seers in the Old Testament, the visions they received, and where each can be found in Scripture.

Chasing Fire

Name	Occupation	Visions	Scripture
Samuel	A servant in the Temple, Priest, Judge of Israel	The demise of Eli, the High Priest, and sons.	1 Sam. 3:10-15, 9:9-19; 1 Chron. 9:22, 26:28, 29:29
Zadok	Chief Priest		2 Sam. 15:27
Gad	Governmental Advisor	The choices of the Lord's punishment for King David	1 Sam. 22:5; 2 Sam. 24:11-13; 1 Sam. 22:5; 2 Sam. 24:11-13; 1 Chron. 21:9, 29:29; 2 Chron. 29:25
Heman	Musician, Songwriter		1 Chron. 15:19, 16:41-42, 25:1,5-6; 2 Chron. 35:15
Iddo	Historian, Author, Priest		2 Chron. 9:29, 12:15, 13:22
Hanani	Unknown	Wars of King Asa	2 Chron. 16:7-10, 19:2
Asaph	Musician, Songwriter	Israel's rebellion, destruction, repentance and restoration; conspiracy against Israel	1 Chron. 15:19, 25:1,6; 2 Chron. 29:30, 35:15; Psalm 50, 73-83
Jeduthun	Chief Musician		1 Chron. 25:1, 2 Chron. 35:15
Amos	Herdsman, tender of sycamore fruit	Swarm of locusts destroying the land, destruction by fire, the plumb line and the Lord standing by the altar	Amos 1:1, 7:12, 7:14, 7:1-9; 8:1-14; 9:1

Many churches across the United States do not discuss this supernatural ability as frequently or with the same tenacity as they teach the basic message of Jesus' birth, death, and resurrection for salvation. However, it is just as true and relevant. It is another way God chooses to communicate with us. And it is necessary for the health and success of the mission of the body of Christ, His bride.

The Seer is gifted with revelation from the Lord by seeing what He is doing or about to do. This knowledge comes through a vision of the night, as with Daniel, or in an open-eye vision in the day, as with Ezekiel and Stephen, the first martyr in Acts.

> *In the first year of Belshazzar king of Babylon, Daniel had a dream and visions of his head while on his bed. Then he wrote down the dream telling the main facts* (Daniel 7:1, NKJV).

> *Now it came to pass in the thirtieth year, in the fourth month, on the fifth day of the month, as I was among the captives by the River Chebar, that the heavens were opened and I saw visions of God* (Ezekiel 1:1, NKJV).

Seers are prophetic. They are given insight, knowledge, or wisdom they could not have unless the Holy Spirit revealed it to them. Prophetic people are merely mail deliverers with a message from the Lord to an individual or group. The seer gets the message in the form of pictures. Jim W. (James) Goll has been a strong prophetic voice in the body of Christ. In his book *The Seer*, he explains:

Chasing Fire

Generally speaking, seers are people who see visions in a consistent and regular manner. For the most part, their prophetic anointing is more visionary than auditory. Rather than receiving words that they attempt to repeat or flow with, they often see pictures that they then describe. These pictures may be in the form of waking visions, or as dreams while sleeping.

The purpose of the message is to bring warning, edification, exhortation, correction, or encouragement to a person, church, city, state, region, or nation.

Jim W. Goll further states:

This dream and vision anointing is to awaken the people of God to the spirit realm. It is a miraculous manifestation of the Spirit that creatively illuminates truth and can confirm the direction of God that has been given to others.

The bottom line is that this gift and all other gifts should point to God, which is the element that is missing in our world of entertainment. It is also the litmus test regarding all things revelatory and any manifestation deemed from the Holy Spirit. The purpose should point the individual or group to God and Christ, and all the glory will go to the Lord.

Many have heard of this and have familiarity with words like *seer* and *prophetic* and may have heard of Jim Goll. On the other hand, many of us have not. Be encouraged to read and study the word for yourself. I accept these things because I have read about them in scripture and have experienced them. When exposed to this spiritual gift, I have seen it happen with order, appropriately, and with attention drawn to God and Christ rather than to the seer.

I have also seen some things that were not the Lord, which is the reason why discernment and knowing the Word of God are imperative. Discernment comes partially from studying and meditating on God's Word and prayer. The following questions are submitted by Jim Goll in his book to discern what is God in the spirit realm.

1. Am I regularly studying the Scriptures (meaning the Bible?)
2. Am I maintaining a life of prayer?
3. Am I seeking purity, cleansing, and holiness in my life?
4. Am I a worshipful member of a local Christian congregation?
5. Am I committed to a few peer relationships that can speak into my life?

All the above questions should be answered yes. If we know God's Word, pray, live a life following God's guidelines, serve regularly, and have accountability with other believers, we will know if what we are seeing or experiencing is from God. Our vertical relationship with God is important, but the Lord has also called us into relationship with each other.

Chasing Fire

For as the body is one and has many members, but all the members of that one body, being many, are one body, so also is Christ. For by one Spirit we were all baptized into one body—whether Jews or Greeks, whether slaves or free—and have all been made to drink into one Spirit (1 Corinthians 12:12-13, NKJV).

And if one member suffers, all the members suffer with it; or if one member is honored, all the members rejoice with it. Now you are the body of Christ, and members individually (1 Corinthians 12:26-27, NKJV).

Though I have been a member of churches that teach and disciple on the supernatural, I have also been a member of churches that do not. All agree on the pillars of the Christian faith: God is the sole creator of the universe. Jesus is His one and only Son who died on the cross for the remission of sin and then was resurrected, soon to return. The Holy Spirit is the great teacher and guide to all regarding God's plan for us, corporately and individually. But the details of how the Holy Spirit does the teaching, leading, and guiding is where disagreement exists.

Family is not much different from the family of God. We argue and have times we don't get along, just like a regular family. We talk about decisions the leadership has made and whether we think they are great or not, just as siblings discuss parents. But in our hearts, we love each other. We pray for each other and support each other. For example, Rick Warren, pastor of Saddleback Church in Southern California and author of the best-selling book, *The Purpose Driven Life,* lost his son to suicide. Throughout social media, the body of Christ posted reminders to pray for Pastor Warren and his family. Not everyone who posted agrees with all his theology, but all love him as a brother in Christ.

I attend a church right now with members who are not going to agree with everything written in this book. Some are irritated with my style of worship in the sanctuary, with hands lifted high. Others are irritated that I respond back to my pastor with "Amen!" during the sermon. Likewise, I am irritated that some of my church family don't raise the roof during praise and worship or shout back to the preacher when he gives an awesome word. Yet there we are, serving together, praying together and eating together, hugging each other, and blessing each other.

If we are to thrive, the body of Christ is necessary for many reasons. One is to offer accountability and keep us from being deceived in spiritual matters. If you believe God has given you a seer or prophetic gifting, you should have answered yes to all the above questions, and you should have evidence of the gifting. If someone declares to you a message from the Lord via a dream or vision, he or she needs to do the same.

The seer gift, like all other spiritual gifts, is given by the Holy Spirit to those He chooses. A person's title, rank, age, nationality, race, level of ability, economic status, level of popularity, gender, etc. do not dictate who gets what. The Lord has even used people not known as His followers to receive messages in dreams and visions. In Matthew, Pilate (the governor who was asked by the religious leaders to have Jesus crucified) was given a warning from his wife.

Chasing Fire

While he was sitting on the judgment seat, his wife sent to him, saying, "Have nothing to do with that just Man, for I have suffered many things today in a dream because of Him" (Matthew 27:19, NKJV).

The word "dream" in this text comes from the Greek word *onar*, meaning a common dream. The context of the word *today* in the above verse refers to the night just passed. God gave a message not only to an unbeliever but a woman regarding the Messiah in a dream. Pontius Pilate listened to his wife and heeded her words by trying to wash his hands of the execution after the crowd cried for the release of Barabbas, a murderer, instead of freeing Christ (Matthew 27:15-26).

The only qualification for receiving this gift is that it is given by the Lord God via the Holy Spirit. So a seer can be any person on the planet. Their race, age, gender, genealogy, occupation, level of education, socio-economic status, height, weight, hair color, and eye color do not matter. All that matters is that God called him or her to it.

God is not boring. Some Christians have decided to live a boring life instead of an abundant one, but God wants to give us the time of our life for our entire life if we let Him. Serving Him and embracing the power of the Holy Spirit is like a roller-coaster ride. There are slow times, fast times, twists, turns, and upside-down times, peaks and lows. And it is so fun!

As for the don'ts, well, the do's far outweigh them. If we focus on accomplishing the do's, we won't have time for the don'ts. And frankly, we won't want to. The flames of our heart turn to meet the flames from God's heart. An expectation and love for participating in His curriculum of teaching, leading, and guiding burns in our souls as our hearts become one with His.

Those with a seeing gift need to be in a body of believers in which discipleship and accountability can take place. Obviously this does not include those who are on hallucinogens or suffer from a mental illness that causes illusions. There are legitimate illnesses and demonic forces that can cause people to "see" things. But we refer to those who are mentally healthy and are not on drugs. Write your visions down and share them with someone you can trust. Visions tend to be more literal, so if your visions are coming true, don't worry. You will know that you are not crazy, and God has chosen to reveal things to you.

Since the seer gift has to do with dreams and visions, let's take a deeper look at them.

Ten

Dreams and Visions

TESTIMONY

I was born into a Catholic family and attended Mass and Sunday school in my early childhood years until my brother was born. Even in the midst of religion and the idea that God existed, I experienced a lot of pain. This pain, in addition to my father's alcoholism and verbal abuse toward my mother, continually chipped away at my faith and belief in God. My family attended church, but I never saw them pray or read the Word. God started to become unreal to me.

When a close friend died of leukemia at the age of nineteen, I made a declaration and held to it: God does not exist and I am an atheist. Soon after, I was on a road to destruction, embarking on a hard and fast lifestyle.

Even though I quit God, He did not quit me. Looking back, I see He was there all along, working to bring me back to Him. I knew it was true when I moved to Austin, Texas, and found myself surrounded by Christian neighbors. This was timely because my heart was empty, and I was longing for something more. My next-door neighbor, Amy, took an interest in me, and we developed a friendship. Though she knew my struggles, she did not judge me.

One night I called Amy, brokenhearted over a break-up with a boyfriend. I was attached not only to him but also to his two children. She listened to me, prayed for me, and invited me to come with her to church the next day. At this point, I had nothing to lose, so I accepted the invitation. The night before we went, I had a dream.

I dreamed that I was in a dingy and dirty home. I saw ten or fifteen people walking around aimlessly in the home, hands to their sides, not saying a word. I recognized an ex-boyfriend, Ben, who was Jewish, and my parents. At a short distance, I saw a white stand-alone tub with a white shower curtain around it. A man opened the shower curtain, looked at me, and said, "Come here."

The water in the shower was running. I got in with him, and when I did, I felt as though the water was pouring over me in buckets. My hair was all in my face, and it was hard to breathe. As I pulled my hair back out of my face, the man gave me a kiss. This was not a sexual kiss but a kiss that was so intense it took my breath away.

Then I gasped. Unsure, I said nothing and paused. He then kissed me again to make sure I un-

Chasing Fire

derstood, and I gasped again. I began to thank him for the kiss, and he said, "This is a gift."

Then I woke up, flooded with emotion. The holiness and purity of the kiss in the dream was vivid. It was real. On the way to church, I told my new friend, Amy, the dream.

We got to church and after what I know now is praise and worship, the pastor got up and said, "Welcome. Today we are going to find out what your dreams mean. What does it mean when you dream about water?"

Wide-eyed, I looked at Amy as the pastor continued. "If you are dreaming about water, it means God is cleansing you, as though you are being baptized. All things are in the past, and you become a new creation in Christ."

My eyes filled with tears, and at that moment, what I know now to be the Holy Spirit came over me, and I knew what the dream meant. I knew without a doubt that Jesus was my Savior and that He visited me in a dream. The holy, pure kiss was from God.

After this, I dove into the word of God and attended church and Bible studies. As I got further into studying God's Word, I learned more about the details of my dream. The people around me were people in my life who had hurt me, and the dirty room was how I felt about my past. The man in the tub was Jesus, giving me the kiss of His love, giving in me the Holy Spirit.

His words to me, "This is a gift," were exactly

right. It was the precious gift of salvation! I went from being an atheist to a believer in Christ overnight. Ephesians 2:8 (NIV) says, "For it is by grace you have been saved, through faith—and this is not from yourselves, it is the gift of God." Oh how I love you too, Lord!

—*Roxanne Lowrance, Real Estate Agent*

For God may speak in one way, or in another, yet man does not perceive it. In a dream, in a vision of the night, when deep sleep falls upon men, while slumbering on their beds, then He opens the ears of men and seals their instruction (Job 33:14-16, NKJV).

A dream can stick like skin. It never leaves and is ever-present. A dream can attach to the mind and mold into the fabric of your being. The events experienced while in deep slumber stay with you. Days, weeks, months, even years go by, and the dream is as if it occurred the night before. For some, dawn has new meaning with a dream that won't leave their thoughts. Acting as dew, it can bring new life to endeavors or aspirations. Or it may shed light on past, present, or future circumstances that directly involve you—or not.

Remember that a seer is someone who sees consistently. On a regular basis, the seer receives visions and/or dreams for the edification of the body. The information may also be given to direct the seer's prayers for someone or some group. The revelation is for the service to others, not only for themselves. So you may not be a seer, but God may choose to communicate to you through a dream or a vision.

For centuries, people have been fascinated with the dream state, and the topic has been discussed among psychologists for decades. Dreams can be a result of what we focused on in the waking hours, a mere reflection of passions in hot pursuit, a tragic event, or our daily job. However, they can also be messages that transcend reason and result in revelation from One who knows all and uses the sleep state to bring information for warning or blessing. The dream is a message from God to you or others.

Dreams are powerful. They can bring gripping fear, renewed hope, or ecstasy in the waking moment. They can bring focused pondering and fill our minds with questions that demand answers. Instant awareness or the need for understanding can come with a dream. Knowing it can be more than just a dream may not be enough. The quest begins with the question, "What does it mean?"

The best example of desperation for meaning is the account of King Nebuchadnezzar of the Babylonian empire found in Daniel chapter two. He was a mighty king of a beautiful and luxurious kingdom. But he had a dream that could have drastic implications if his magicians, sorcerers, and astrologers were not able to find the meaning. He demanded that they tell the dream first and then interpret it. Only then would he be satisfied that the interpretation was accurate. If they were unable, the king would have all of them cut in pieces and their houses made an ash heap.

Fortunately, Daniel, who was chosen by the king as more wise than all his magicians, sorcerers, and astrologers, had the answer. After praying to God, Daniel received the revelation in a night vision.

Dreams and Visions

He went before King Nebuchadnezzar and said, "... The secret which the king has demanded, the wise men, the astrologers, the magicians, and the soothsayers cannot declare to the king. But there is a God in heaven who reveals secrets, and He has made known to King Nebuchadnezzar what will be in the latter days." (Daniel 2:27-28a, NKJV), and Daniel revealed the king's dream and its meaning

There are many other biblical examples of God speaking to people through dreams:

And it happened, at the time when the flocks conceived, that I lifted my eyes and saw in a dream, and behold, the rams which leaped upon the flocks were streaked, speckled, and gray-spotted (Genesis 31:10, NKJV).

But God had come to Laban the Syrian in a dream by night, and said to him, "Be careful that you speak to Jacob neither good nor bad" (Genesis 31:24, NKJV).

Then the butler and the baker of the king of Egypt, who were confined in the prison, had a dream, both of them, each man's dream in one night and each man's dream with its own interpretation (Genesis 40:5, NKJV).

And when Gideon had come, there was a man telling a dream to his companion. He said, "I have had a dream: To my surprise, a loaf of barley bread tumbled into the camp of Midian; it came to a tent and struck it so that it fell and overturned, and the tent collapsed." Then his

115

Chasing Fire

companion answered and said, "This is nothing else but the sword of Gideon the son of Joash, a man of Israel! Into his hand God has delivered Midian and the whole camp." And so it was, when Gideon heard the telling of the dream and its interpretation, that he worshiped. He returned to the camp of Israel, and said, "Arise, for the Lord has delivered the camp of Midian into your hand" (Judges 7:13-15, NKJV).

While he was sitting on the judgment seat, his wife sent to him, saying, "Have nothing to do with that just Man, for I have suffered many things today in a dream because of Him" (Matthew 27:19, NKJV).

Now Joseph had a dream, and he told it to his brothers; and they hated him even more (Genesis 37:5, NKJV).

Hated him? Joseph was Jacob's favorite son. The dream was a prophetic dream that spoke to Joseph's greatness over his brothers. Interestingly, when Joseph shared the dream, his brothers knew exactly what it meant. It brought them to a murderous jealousy.

The moral of Joseph's testimony is to be careful with whom we share a dream. We should use wisdom when secrets are revealed to us about our life. They are pearls from heaven to us from God. A dream like this is meant to encourage us and give us a glimpse into understanding the plan and destiny He has for us.

Dreams and Visions

Do not give what is holy to the dogs; nor cast your pearls before swine, lest they trample them under their feet, and turn and tear you in pieces (Matthew 7:6, NKJV).

Have you ever slouched in your seat, closed your eyes, and covered your face with your hand? This was my position when our mortgage company revealed its failure to close escrow on our new home—only two weeks before our closing.

My husband and I immediately cried out to the One directing our path and calling us to move. For me, it would be the second time to Austin, Texas. That night, the Captain of our ship answered me in a dream.

I dreamed I was walking through a wheat field, heading toward the horizon. Suddenly, three pitch-black tornadoes came from my right in the distance to block my way. Destructive and dangerous, they left me no way to reach the place where I needed to be.

Then, from my left came a soft, clear tornado with beautiful golden leaves swirling gently inside. It danced toward the black tornadoes, its strength stopping them from moving. At the left of this movement of protection was a clear way to my destination. Then I woke up.

Like Joseph's brothers, I knew exactly what the dream meant. Upon waking, I told my husband that God was going to provide a different way. The power of the Holy Spirit came upon me, and I immediately got online and started looking for other title and mortgage companies.

Chasing Fire

Three of them stuck out to me. I made the first call and got a voice message. At the sound of the agent's voice, I knew by divine revelation that he was the person the Lord would use.

By faith, I e-mailed the current company and gave thanks to the agent for working with us and doing all they could. I also said that I was a woman of faith, and the Lord promised us this home but was going to use a different vessel to accomplish His plan.

The man on the message did turn out to be the vessel God chose. From the day we spoke with him to closing was ten days—an early closing. Today, my husband and I still live in that home the Lord promised us. Glory to God!

The purpose of this dream, in my opinion, was multi-faceted. One, it was an encouragement to know that God was working and had the way for us to move. Two, it was for my husband, the pastor and leader of our home, who also was waiting on a sign. Three, it was for you. If not for the dream and our obedience to the message of the dream, I would not be in a position to write this book, which is for everyone to know that God loves us and wants to have a two-way dialogue with us. He is a supernatural being living in another dimension. He will use supernatural ways, such as a dream, to communicate with us. It is wise to pay attention to our dreams, especially to the following, which are highly likely to be messages from God:

- Dreams that stick with you, maybe for years
- Dreams that have occurred more than once, a reoccurring dream

Dreams and Visions

- Dreams within a dream. This happens when you awaken while dreaming, but you are still dreaming and then wake for real.

Sometimes God uses visions as a means of communication. Visions are different from dreams. Dreams are more metaphorical, while visions are literal. Dreams can bring messages relating to the past, present, or future. Visions usually relate to the future or seeing a spiritual being, such as an angel or Jesus.

Now after six days Jesus took Peter, James, and John his brother, led them up on a high mountain by themselves; and He was transfigured before them. His face shone like the sun, and His clothes became as white as the light. And behold, Moses and Elijah appeared to them, talking with Him (Matthew 17:1-3, NKJV).

This account in Matthew was a vision experienced by Peter, James, and John. While awake, they saw Jesus in His glorified state, along with Moses and Elijah, who lived thousands of years prior. At the end of the experience, Jesus commanded them not to share the vision with anyone until after His resurrection.

Daniel saw an angel in a vision (Daniel 8:15-16), and Zacharias, the father of John the Baptist, saw a vision of an angel in the temple (Luke 1:11-22).

The Lord can bring a vision in several different states.

Chasing Fire

1. A trance (Greek: *ekstasis*) This word is used three times in the New King James Version, each time in the book of Acts. The literal meaning of the ekstasis in the verses below is the same for each use. It occurs when a man, by some sudden emotion, is transported, as it were, out of himself. In this rapt condition, although he is awake, his mind is drawn away from all surrounding objects and wholly fixed on things divine. He sees nothing but the forms and images lying within and thinks that he perceives with his bodily eyes and ears the realities shown him by God.

I was in the city of Joppa praying; and in a trance I saw a vision, an object descending like a great sheet, let down from heaven by four corners; and it came to me (Acts 11:5, NKJV).

Then he became very hungry and wanted to eat; but while they made ready, he fell into a trance and saw heaven opened and an object like a great sheet bound at the four corners, descending to him and let down to the earth. In it were all kinds of four-footed animals of the earth, wild beasts, creeping things, and birds of the air. And a voice came to him, "Rise, Peter; kill and eat." Now while Peter wondered within himself what this vision which he had seen meant, behold, the men who had been sent from Cornelius had made inquiry for Simons house, and stood before the gate (Acts 10:10-13,17, NKJV).

Dreams and Visions

Now it happened, when I returned to Jerusalem and was praying in the temple, that I was in a trance and saw Him saying to me, "Make haste and get out of Jerusalem quickly, for they will not receive your testimony concerning Me" (Acts 22:17-18, NKJV).

2. In a dream, like Daniel

3. While awake, like Zacharias and the three disciples at the Mount of Transfiguration

God uses dreams and visions to talk to us. He wants to convey His message to us so we can know what He is doing. God is gracious and compassionate. In order for us to know His plan for us, He has to give it. That means he must speak, and we must hear.

God chooses the recipient of His messages in dreams and visions. When we were being formed in the womb, the Lord decided what gifts we would have, how they should be used, and when. In addition, the Lord declares in His Word:

And it shall come to pass in the last days, says God, that I will pour out of My Spirit on all flesh; your sons and your daughters shall prophesy, your young men shall see visions, your old men shall dream dreams (Acts 2:17, NKJV).

This scripture says He will pour out His Spirit on "all flesh"—saved, unsaved, pew warmer, Jesus freak; it doesn't

Chasing Fire

matter. God will pour His spirit on all flesh, and people will have dreams and visions. For the record, when translated from Greek and Hebrew, the phrases *young men* and *old men* in the verse above mean, "young people or youth" and "someone advanced in life." Gender and age have nothing to do with this form of communication from God.

But how do we know if our dream is from God and not the pizza we had the night before? And if it is from God, how do we find the meaning? If you wake and you don't remember your dream, then according to Job 33:14-16, it is sealed-up instruction that He will unseal in His time. If after you awaken, the dream feels as if it actually happened, if it is a reoccurring dream, or if it is cemented in your mind, it is possibly a dream or vision from God. At this point, you need an interpreter.

Ask God to send the interpretation Himself (via His voice, divine knowledge, His Word) or through one of His servants. Almost all the knowledge I have gleaned regarding dreams and visions comes from sitting under the teaching of Streams Ministries and its founder, John Paul Jackson. His ministry offers courses specifically related to hearing God, dreams and visions, miracles, and supernatural living. I am certified to teach two of his courses, but they are also available online with him as the teacher. In addition, some Bible-based churches with a prophetic ministry can help.

The Bible is more than just the Ten Commandments. We cannot rely on clergy, a pastor, a priest, our Sunday school teacher or anyone in full-time ministry to tell us about everything in the world's bestseller. I have been studying God's Word for twenty years now, have been in church almost every Sunday, have a great pastor who preaches the whole truth and nothing but the truth, and I teach the Word to others. Yet I have only begun to scratch the surface. We have to read and study it for ourselves.

There is much in that book! Drama, heartache, victory, loss, conspiracy, and power come through the pages that have transcended time. Today's reality shows have nothing on the historical record and testimonies outlined in the Bible. It's the best unscripted reality, and it's supernaturally real. The best part is that the testament is not over. God's plan is being played out today. It is all being written in books placed on the shelves of heaven.

> *And I saw the dead, the great and the small, standing before the throne, and books were opened; and another book was opened, which is the book of life; and the dead were judged from the things which were written in the books, according to their deeds* (Revelation 20:12, NASB).

What is your testimony? What does the Lord have in store for you? If you do not know, ask Him. Maybe He will bring the answer through a dream or vision.

Eleven

Knowing the Unknown

Surely, the Lord God does nothing, unless He reveals His secret to His servants the prophets (Amos 3:7, NKJV).

Have you ever seen wind knock someone down to the ground—inside a building? Many, many years ago, I was at a church conference that featured a man revered as a prophet in the body of Christ. Kim Clement was on stage, speaking a message from the word of God regarding the church we were in. God used him to encourage the pastor, the leadership, and the flock. At the end of the message, he announced that God was going to minister to people individually.

This man, by nothing other than the Spirit of the Lord, started calling people out of the audience by name and/or their home address. Even though this is the first time he had been in the area, he was able to describe the homes of the people God intended to reach. He would describe

Knowing the Unknown

someone's physical features and what they were wearing to bring them to the front of the stage. I had not witnessed anything like this in my life. I'm an extrovert and talker who will shout back to the preacher with "amen." In awe, all I could do was watch, gasp, and drop my jaw.

There had to be at least two thousand people in the building. People came from all over the San Francisco Bay area to see him. At first thought, due to the sheer unlikelihood of pinpoint accuracy without God, I believed He was being used by the Lord. Then another thought came: This dude is just like all those movies of counterfeits. All these people are paid to put on a show.

God corrected this thought with a supernatural, I-AM-in-the-house-so-don't-get-it-twisted moment. At one point, Kim Clement said that the Lord wanted to minister to a lady and her daughter. He pointed to a section of the sanctuary and said, "You are sitting in this area." Then he gave the woman's address, described her home, and named the city it was in.

Soon the woman came forward with her daughter. Kim Clement told her that the Lord had something for her, but he didn't know what it was. He instructed her to stand in the middle of the stage with her daughter and wait. He then turned around to minister to more people in the audience. Before he could speak the first sentence, a wind came through the wall, across to middle stage, knocked over the woman and daughter, and quickly doubled back like a hand to cradle the fall.

Some people gasped, some people screamed, some did both and started pointing at them. The response of the

Chasing Fire

crowd caused Kim Clement to turn around, only to find the woman and the girl on the floor, out cold. They lay there with their eyes closed, as if they were asleep. And they stayed that way for about fifteen minutes.

When the two sat up, Kim Clement asked what happened. The woman explained that she saw Jesus in a vision. He spoke to her and said all was going to be well.

I don't remember this woman's name or her complete testimony of what the Lord did that night. My heart was struck with something else. I learned that God isn't off in heaven somewhere in the corner of the universe, doing nothing but wait for things to play out. He is active. Also, I discovered that He uses men to reveal the unknown to others.

After I saw this gentleman, the Lord opened doors for me to stand before other men and women with the gift of prophecy. I have seen God use these servants of the Lord to encourage others, interpret dreams, and predict future events that have since come to pass.

A great example of future events being prophesied was done by John Paul Jackson. In 2008, he released a DVD called *The Perfect Storm*, in which he shared the word of the Lord that came to him regarding the future. One of those prophecies was that a terrorist leadership would take the place of Egyptian President Hosni Mubarak. Three years later, in 2011, President Mubarak was forced into resignation, and Muhammad Morsi of the Muslim Brotherhood became the new president in 2012. The Muslim Brotherhood has been known to use acts of terror to further their cause. After his installment, President Morsi said

Knowing the Unknown

things that made him more like a dictator than a president. Some of the prophecies in this recording have happened, some are playing out today, and others are still to come.

A *prophet* is a man divinely inspired by the Holy Spirit to speak His message to leaders, nations, states, cities, churches, and individuals and/or foretell future events concerning His plan. This man is gifted to receive and share divine revelation and secrets from the Lord as He directs him. A *prophetess* is the same as a prophet, except she is a woman. A *prophecy* is the divinely inspired word spoken or written by the prophet or prophetess. To prophesy is to speak or write a prophetic word by divine inspiration.

The Lord began to introduce me to His servants, the prophets, in 1994. It's been twenty years, and I can't count how many spot-on words of knowledge, wisdom, and divine revelation I have heard. I am thankful to the Lord for giving me the ability to see this gift function properly in the body, with order and accountability. However, my experiences do not validate their validity. The prophecies are the word of God. This gift and role are seen throughout the entire text of scripture.

The majority of biblical text is prophetic in nature. The Bible that most evangelical Christians read consists of sixty-six books. Of these, sixteen are authored by and named after a prophet. Moses, considered to be a prophet, wrote the Pentateuch, the first five books of the Bible. The book of Revelation is the testimony of John's visions and recorded prophecies of the end times. Only two chapters of the twenty-one in Revelation are letters from the Lord to seven churches. Some believe these letters serve a dual pur-

Chasing Fire

pose: as letters to actual churches at that time, and as a prophetic voice to the same types of churches that exist even today. Below is the number of times that words regarding this subject are used in scripture.

	Times used in NKJV	Times used in NIV	Times used in NAS	Times used in NLT
Prophet	243	253	236	239
Prophets	237	248	238	264
Prophetess	8	1	8	0
Prophesy	86	66	75	55
Prophesying	9	32	24	16
Prophecy	18	44	19	42

In addition, the four gospels of the New Testament (Matthew, Mark, Luke, and John) are filled with prophecy, starting with revelation regarding the births and lives of John the Baptist and Jesus. Matthew, Mark, and Luke contain Jesus' prophecies regarding end-time events and His second coming. The book of Esther does not mention God's name. Yet this book holds a strong prophetic word and warning delivered to this queen:

> *And Mordecai told them to answer Esther: "Do not think in your heart that you will escape in the king's palace any more than all the other Jews. For if you remain completely silent at this time, relief and deliverance will arise for the Jews from another place, but you and your father's house will perish. Yet who knows*

whether you have come to the kingdom for such a time as this?" (Esther 4:13-14, NKJV)

Consider the verse in the beginning of this chapter:

Surely the Lord God does nothing, unless He reveals His secret to His servants the prophets (Amos 3:7, NKJV).

If God has no prophets, then He is doing nothing—not answering prayer, giving direction in our life, setting up kingdoms, rulers, and all the authorities from the least to the greatest, or speaking. We are told that Jesus makes intercession for us in heaven. If God stops speaking and does nothing, there is no more to be done. Jesus should not be making intercession for us. He does only what He sees His father in heaven doing. So if God stops, so does Christ and His prayers for us.

Who is he who condemns? It is Christ who died, and furthermore is also risen, who is even at the right hand of God, who also makes intercession for us (Romans 8:34, NKJV).

Let every soul be subject to the governing authorities. For there is no authority except from God, and the authorities that exist are appointed by God (Romans 13:1, NKJV).

The king's heart is in the hand of the Lord, like the rivers of water; He turns it wherever He wishes (Proverbs 21:1, NKJV).

Chasing Fire

Then Jesus answered and said to them, "Most assuredly, I say to you, the Son can do nothing of Himself, but what He sees the Father do; for whatever He does, the Son also does in like manner" (John 5:19, NKJV).

Let's look at the following verses:

And God has appointed these in the church: first apostles, second prophets, third teachers, after that miracles, then gifts of healings, helps, administrations, varieties of tongues (1 Corinthians 12:28, NKJV).

And He Himself gave some to be apostles, some prophets, some evangelists, and some pastors and teachers, for the equipping of the saints for the work of ministry, for the edifying of the body of Christ, till we all come to the unity of the faith and of the knowledge of the Son of God, to a perfect man, to the measure of the stature of the fullness of Christ; that we should no longer be children, tossed to and fro and carried about with every wind of doctrine, by the trickery of men, in the cunning craftiness of deceitful plotting, but, speaking the truth in love, may grow up in all things into Him who is the head—Christ—from whom the whole body, joined and knit together by what every joint supplies, according to the effective working by which every part does its share, causes growth of the body for the edifying of itself in love (Ephesians 4:11-16, NKJV).

The apostle Paul, in 1 Corinthians 12:12-27, relays the necessity of the body parts functioning for the benefit of

Knowing the Unknown

the whole body. He further explains that it is ridiculous for one part to deem another unnecessary. Through Paul, the Spirit of the Lord is speaking to the church regarding the gifts of the Spirit and roles God appointed in the church.

In the Corinthians verse, we read what God has appointed, and in Ephesians 4:11, we gain understanding of the roles Christ gave. Throughout Christianity, evangelists, pastors, and teachers are accepted as roles to be filled in the body of Christ today. In every church, there will be at least one pastor and teacher. Some churches have evangelists, even though they might not have that title. This is not the case with apostles and prophets. Some churches have men and women functioning in this role, and others do not.

When looking at the phrases "God has appointed" and "He Himself gave" in the above scriptures, a question arises. If God ended the use of one of them, then why not the others? To say that apostles and prophets exist no longer is like taking a marker and blotting out those words right after the phrases, "God has appointed" and "He Himself gave."

After looking at Ephesians 4:11-16, we read that these functions should take place until "we all come to the unity of the faith and of the knowledge of the Son of God, to a perfect man, to the measure of the stature of the fullness of Christ" (verse 13). Since this verse has not been fulfilled, all those roles must be functioning today.

Where is the truth in this subject? God's Word promises that if we ask for wisdom, God will grant it. In the same Word, Christ says that He is truth and that the Spirit of God will lead us into all truth. If we ask Him for

Chasing Fire

the truth, He will reveal it to us. And much of His truth is in the Bible.

> *However, when He, the Spirit of truth, has come, He will guide you into all truth; for He will not speak on His own authority, but whatever He hears He will speak; and He will tell you things to come* (John 16:13, NKJV).

In the above verse, Jesus clearly tells us that the Holy Spirit will speak truth to us according to what He hears from God, including things to come. In other words, the Holy Spirit will relay future events to people. Hearing, receiving, and understanding things to come and then sharing that information is prophecy.

> *For the Lord gives wisdom; from His mouth come knowledge and understanding* (Proverbs 2:6, NKJV).

> *Ask, and it will be given to you; seek, and you will find; knock, and it will be opened to you. For everyone who asks receives, and he who seeks finds, and to him who knocks it will be opened. Or what man is there among you who, if his son asks for bread, will give him a stone? Or if he asks for a fish, will he give him a serpent? If you then, being evil, know how to give good gifts to your children, how much more will your Father who is in heaven give good things to those who ask Him!* (Matthew 7:7-11, NKJV)

> *Jesus said to him, "I am the way, the truth, and the life.*

No one comes to the Father except through Me" (John 14:6, NKJV).

All Scripture is given by inspiration of God, and is profitable for doctrine, for reproof, for correction, for instruction in righteousness, that the man of God may be complete, thoroughly equipped for every good work (2 Timothy 3:16-17, NKJV).

Be encouraged. We all have a dynamic role to play in God's Kingdom. He has endowed us with supernatural spiritual gifts. When we are faithful and obedient to use them according to His purpose, He will be right there with His support. Our divine encounter with God then gives opportunity for others to have an encounter with God as well. Our little step of faith in sharing a word precedes a spectacular show of His hand on the lives of others for His glory. Revelation 19:10 says, "… the testimony of Jesus is the spirit of prophecy." Prophecy is a form of communication the Lord has been using from the Garden of Eden until now. He speaks these messages to an individual, either for that person's life or for someone else's. Prophecy is real, alive, and for today—for all of us!

Twelve

Servants From Heaven

TESTIMONY

I compare myself to Jonathan in the Bible when getting direction from the Lord or staying in His will. When trying to determine whether God wants me to do a particular thing, I ask the Lord to let it happen if it's His will. Then I pray that if it's not His will, he will close the doors. Next, I wait and see what He does. This is how I got to China. He opened the doors for me to go, so I went.

My intent was to find English-speaking Christians and then go into North Korea so I could have an understanding of how things work and where my experience could be of use. Once in the Province Jilin, I found out that I could find English-speaking Christians at a university. When I went to look for the university, I couldn't find it. I searched for four hours, but it was nowhere to be found. So I thought maybe this wasn't right and decided to come back to the States. I went to the bus stop.

Servants From Heaven

There I saw a man—a white man with white hair. He looked American. So I approached him and struck up a conversation. He shared a little about himself, and I told him how I wasn't able to find the university and that it seemed as though there was nothing for me here, so I was returning home.

But this guy knew about the university and thought I should go there. He gave me the exact location of the school and directions to it. There were people there, he said, who could help me, and I merely needed to speak to whoever was in charge.

I immediately headed for the university. I asked for the English Department and waited around for a while. Then someone took me to a lady who had been serving in South Korea. She offered me a teaching position and introduced me to the president of the school that day.

Everything happened just as the white-haired man said. I asked around about him so I could find him and let him know everything had worked out. I asked students, the lady who hired me, and the president of the school. I even asked around town. No one knew who I was talking about. No one had seen a white man in this town. He was nowhere to be found, and no one else had seen him. Everyone who hears this story says, "That was an angel!"

I asked if he believes the white-haired man was an angel. He said, "I have no doubt it was an angel!"

—*Brian Stewart, Engineer*

Chasing Fire

Do not forget to entertain strangers, for by so doing some have unwittingly entertained angels (Hebrews 13:2, NKJV).

Instead of the break of dawn or the sweet sound of God's voice, footsteps in my bathroom awakened me in the middle of the night. My eleven-year-old thinking surmised the steps were my father's. I rolled over to see what was happening, and I realized I could see perfectly without my glasses.

My hearing adjusted and the steps became louder. They seemed to be pacing back and forth in my bathroom, which shared a wall with my bedroom. As I sat up in bed and gazed through my bedroom door, I beheld a black shadow cast on the wall by the bathroom light. It was shaped like a short man wearing a top hat. At the sight, fear entered me because my father was over six feet tall and did not own a top hat. Knowledge of an intruder brought forth a gasp.

Then the shadow peeled from the wall and started toward my bedroom door. This was evil. Having already learned that God is bigger than the boogeyman and that Jesus destroys darkness, it came to my mind to call on the name of the King of Kings. In a small but confident whisper, I called to Him in a rapid, staccato tempo. "Jesus! Jesus! Jesus!"

Immediately, twelve white light beings dropped through my bedroom ceiling, and each one started waving something around like a sword. The light from these beings and their weapons made the Star Wars light sabers seem cartoonish and dull.

I was young, but I knew there was a fight happening around my bed. And that dark shadow, whoever or whatever it was, lost bitterly. He got utterly destroyed. Then the light beings went back up through the ceiling. And my sight returned to normal. As a child, I was legally blind. Everything became blurry once again. I reached for my glasses, put them on, and began to call very quietly to my mom. She came in and though she was there, I did not go back to sleep the rest of the night.

Angelic encounters are found throughout the Bible. It's interesting that these celestial beings are widely accepted as real in our modern culture. Some people pray to them and treat them as deities, but they aren't. They are created beings just as we are. An accurate definition is given for them in *Hayford's Bible Handbook*:

Angel—a member of an order of heavenly beings who are superior to man in power and intelligence. By nature angels are spiritual beings (Heb. 1:14). Their nature is superior to human nature (Heb. 2:7), and they have superhuman power and knowledge (2 Sam. 14:17, 20; 2 Pet. 2:11). They are not however all-powerful or all-knowing (Ps. 103:20; 2 Thess. 1:7).

We are told in scripture that angels are God's servants. God is their only commander, and they adhere solely to His voice. They serve Him in heaven around the throne, protect people on earth, deliver messages to people regarding God's will, plans, and purpose; and carry out whatever else God

Chasing Fire

commands them to do. Thereby, they are another way God speaks to us. Here are some examples in scripture:

Now an angel of the Lord spoke to Philip, saying, "Arise and go toward the south along the road which goes down from Jerusalem to Gaza ..." (Acts 8:26, NKJV).

But the angel said to him, "Do not be afraid, Zacharias, for your prayer is heard; and your wife Elizabeth will bear you a son, and you shall call his name John" (Luke 1:13, NKJV).

Then the angel said to them, "Do not be afraid, for behold, I bring you good tidings of great joy which will be to all people" (Luke 2:10, NKJV).

Then as he (Elijah) lay and slept under a broom tree, suddenly an angel touched him, and said to him, "Arise and eat" (1 Kings 19:5, NKJV).

But the angel answered and said to the women, "Do not be afraid, for I know that you seek Jesus who was crucified" (Matthew 28:5, NKJV).

My favorite biblical record that reveals the reality of angelic beings is in the New Testament. Peter was in prison for the sake of the gospel and Christ, and an angel broke him out of prison. He then went to a house of believers, who were praying. This is what happened when he knocked on the gate:

Servants From Heaven

And as Peter knocked at the door of the gate, a girl named Rhoda came to answer. When she recognized Peter's voice, because of her gladness she did not open the gate, but ran in and announced that Peter stood before the gate. But they said to her, "You are beside yourself!" Yet she kept insisting that it was so. So they said, "It is his angel" (Acts 12:13-15, NKJV).

When translated from Greek, the word *angel* in the above verse means a messenger, an envoy, one who is sent, an angel, a messenger from God. In this context, it means a heavenly spirit that waits upon the Creator and Ruler of the universe and is sent by Him to earth to execute His purposes. In this particular case, he is a guardian angel. In other words, when the people in the house used this word, they were saying it was a creature from heaven executing the will of almighty God.

The fact that they said it's not Peter but his angel still boggles my mind today. Were angelic visitations that common? Are they today without headliner attention and common discussion? What is the deal with this? I do not know. However, the lesson is simple: God will use angels, these great spirit beings He created, to carry out His purposes, and we should expect it. Below is another interesting account about an angel at the pool of Bethesda.

For an angel went down at a certain time into the pool and stirred up the water; then whoever stepped in first, after the stirring of the water, was made well of whatever disease he had (John 5:4, NKJV).

Chasing Fire

Could you imagine? If that were happening today, with all the diseases that exist, the line would be forever long.

I have a theory. An angel stirring up water is not needed anymore because, after Jesus' death and resurrection, He has given people the gift of healing, through the power of the Holy Spirit. I have been an eyewitness to God using the laying on of hands with a prayer of command to heal people. However, that is another book.

Another interesting event is a conversation that took place between the prophet Daniel and an angel. Daniel had been fasting and praying for three weeks. He was looking for understanding and interceding for Israel. On the twenty-fourth day of his fast and prayer, Daniel had a vision. An angel appeared to him to bring understanding of the last days. This is what the angel said:

> *Then he said to me, "Do not fear, Daniel, for from the first day that you set your heart to understand, and to humble yourself before your God, your words were heard; and I have come because of your words. But the prince of the kingdom of Persia withstood me twenty-one days; and behold, Michael, one of the chief princes, came to help me, for I had been left alone there with the king of Persia. Now I have come to make you understand what will happen to your people in the latter days, for the vision refers to many days yet to come"* (Daniel 10:12-14, NKJV).

Daniel began to pray and fast for more understanding. He repented on behalf of his nation's sin. God sent an angel

Servants From Heaven

to bring the answer to Daniel, but the angel was held up in a battle with the prince of Persia for twenty-one days. Another angel, Michael, came to assist him in the fight so he could be released to bring the message from God.

This is very interesting to me because it brings a little information about how the spiritual realm operates. It tells that the enemy, the devil, has ranks of evil forces that war against the will of God. In addition, even though dark forces war against the will of God and work to attack His children, those forces are no match for the Lord and His angelic army.

Many different types of angelic beings are used by God and serve Him. Seraphim and cherubim serve God around His throne. They give Him worship and praise, continuously crying out, "Holy, Holy, Holy, Lord God Almighty, who was and is and is to come!" (Revelation 4:8b, NKJV). These creatures are winged with four faces and eyes that cover their entire body. Ezekiel, in his throne-room experience, describes them this way:

As for the likeness of the living creatures, their appearance was like burning coals of fire, like the appearance of torches going back and forth among the living creatures. The fire was bright, and out of the fire went lightening. And the living creatures ran back and forth, in appearance like a flash of lightening (Ezekiel 1:13-14 NKJV).

Chasing Fire

We also read about the archangels Michael and Gabriel in scripture. These are high-ranking angels who lead God's angelic army and bring messages to God's people on earth. We read about them in the books of Daniel and Luke. In addition, there are angels who rejoiced while the morning stars sang during the creation of the earth's foundation (Job 38:4,7), watchers who never sleep or rest and carry out administrative duties of God (Daniel 4:13, 17, 23) and the ranks of the devil's angelic force mentioned in Ephesians:

Finally, my brethren, be strong in the Lord and in the power of His might. Put on the whole armor of God, that you may be able to stand against the wiles of the devil. For we do not wrestle against flesh and blood, but against principalities, against powers, against the rulers of the darkness of this age, against spiritual hosts of wickedness in the heavenly places (Ephesians 6:10-12, NKJV).

Angels have an important role in carrying out God's plan for all men on earth and His millennial Kingdom to come, as well as the final destruction of earth and the formation of a new heaven and new earth (Revelation 19-21.) They are His agents who assist us, not our agents who assist Him. Commanding angels is almost like walking onto a military base and telling the soldiers what to do. The Lord commands angels on our behalf. His use of angels to give us messages and protect us makes me think of a verse in Isaiah:

Servants From Heaven

"No weapon formed against you shall prosper, and every tongue which rises against you in judgment you shall condemn. This is the heritage of the servants of the Lord, and their righteousness is from Me," says the Lord (Isaiah 54:17, NKJV).

What an awesome promise from God! This is another extension of His love for us. This love from God is not withheld from anyone who wants it. Reach for Him. Call out to Him. He is here right now, with all of us. He has been there all along. And there are angels He would like you to meet.

Thirteen

The God Zone

There are people who have heard God's audible voice. That means they have heard the voice of God using the physical ear, in the same manner in which you hear another person's voice. There are several instances in the Bible that record God's voice being heard in this capacity:

So the Lord spoke to Moses face to face, as a man speaks to his friend (Exodus 33:11, NKJV).

And suddenly a voice came from heaven, saying, "This is My beloved Son, in whom I am well pleased" (Matthew 3:17, NKJV).

"Father, glorify Your name." Then a voice came from heaven, saying, "I have both glorified it and will glorify it again" (John 12:28, NKJV).

These words the Lord spoke to all your assembly, in the mountain from the midst of the fire, the cloud, and the thick darkness, with a loud voice; and He added no more. And He wrote them on two tablets of stone and gave them to me. So it was, when you heard the voice from the midst of the darkness, while the mountain was burning with fire, that you came near to me, all the heads of your tribes and your elders. And you said: "Surely the Lord our God has shown us His glory and His greatness, and we have heard His voice from the midst of the fire. We have seen this day that God speaks with man; yet he still lives" (Deuteronomy 5:22-24, NKJV)

Why did God speak audibly to some and not others? Honestly, no one can answer that question. He's God. He does what He wants. However, we can look at a possible theory based on the ones He spoke to audibly and what each message was. Let's look at Moses.

Moses had a lot of drama in his life. When he was an infant, his mother placed him in a basket and sent him down the river. This was her attempt to save him from the slaughter of young children commanded by Pharaoh. Miriam, Moses' sister, followed the basket and saw Pharaoh's daughter take him out. Miriam approached the princess and offered to get someone to nurse the baby. Of course, after the princess said yes, Moses' mother took him to nurse until he is older. When he was given to Pharaoh's daughter, she named him Moses.

Later in his adulthood, he witnessed the horror experi-

Chasing Fire

enced by his brethren, the Hebrews. When he saw an Egyptian beating a Hebrew, he took the Egyptian's life and buried him in the sand.

The next day he learned that what he had done was known. He fled to Midian. Decades later, God spoke to Moses, who was now eighty years old. God instructed him to go back to Egypt, tell Pharaoh to let all the Hebrews go, and bring them to the Promised Land.

If we were in Moses' shoes, would a dream or vision be enough to convince us to go back to the place where we were wanted for murder and tell the Pharaoh that God is shutting down the plantation? This would be like dreaming that you are standing in the White House, telling President Obama that God sent you. You command him to restore Gaza and the West Bank to the nation of Israel and to assist Israel in occupying all the land promised to them in God's word. Then you wake up.

Do you adhere to the dream? What do you do? I would roll over and before going back to sleep, I'd say, "Woo! Praise God! That was just a dream, because I know He is not sending me to the White House."

Let's examine another example: Noah. In Genesis 6:13, God spoke to Noah. The text says that God told Noah to build an ark because a great flood would destroy the earth. We must understand that up to this point in history, there had been no rain. Many Bible scholars believe there was a canopy of water separating our inner atmosphere from an outer atmosphere. When the canopy was broken, all the water in the atmosphere flooded the earth.

Also consider the size the ark must have been.

The God Zone

Historians and Bible scholars believe it was huge. Hebrew scholars agree that a cubit (the measure used for building the ark) is about 17½ to 21½ inches long. Therefore, the Ark was about 450 feet long, 75 feet wide, and 45 feet tall. Huge! It is also believed that Noah was between 450 and 500 years old when God told him to build the ark, and it took him about 120 years to complete the project. What would be Noah's best way of knowing that building an ark was God's will? At this time, there were no written scriptures, so would a person as a representative of God suffice?

We can also look at Job. This man not only heard God speak but also had a dialogue with Him. In short, Job was a godly man who had God's favor on his life. Everything Job touched prospered. He was blessed with a wife and many sons and daughters. He was wealthy and successful.

Without Job knowing, God pointed him out to Satan and asked if he has considered him. Satan basically responds, "You give him everything! You have a hedge of protection around him and won't let me touch him. Stretch out Your hand against him and see if he doesn't curse You to your face!"

"Do what you want to him," God said. "Take everything. But you cannot harm him physically."

After losing his property and all his children, Job passed the test and didn't curse God. But Satan convinced God to allow his health to fail as a final test.

Job's friends were convinced his troubles were a result of sin. His wife begged him to curse God and die. But Job never cursed God. He cursed his own birth and regretted the fact that he was alive. He prayed for relief, complained

Chasing Fire

to God about his circumstances, and questioned Him about it. Then, after a long, discouraging discourse with his friends, the Lord answered Job's prayer. In today's language, God asked Job, "Who are you that you should question Me? Get ready, because now I will ask you some questions, and let's see how you answer. Where were you when I laid down the foundations of the earth? Tell me, if you know."

God went on and on, from Chapter 38 through 40:2 without interruption. In verses 4 and 5, Job responded with two short sentences, and God continued from chapter 40:6 thru 41:34. It reminds me of those speeches many of us have received from parents when we questioned their authority. They are the ones that start with, "What were you doing when I was going to work to make sure you had a roof over your head?"

Job repented and God restored him, giving him double of everything he lost. The enemy lost the bet. Job did not curse God, but he questioned God's sovereignty and omnipotence. Think about it: would you rather be rebuked by a friend or have the voice of the Almighty crashing into your circumstances with correction?

Looking at these examples, we can see that when God speaks audibly to a person, there is a lot at stake. Either the recipient needs it due to the significance and weight of their purpose, or correction needs to take place. When God speaks audibly or supernaturally and brings someone to the throne room in heaven, it is just like being called to attention by a person of authority when we don't expect it.

For instance, in school there are teachers, coaches, counselors, administrators, janitors, and a principal. One

The God Zone

day the principal comes to your classroom, interrupts every-thing by calling you out by name, and says, "I need to see you in my office—now."

Bringing this supernatural occurrence to a natural one, what would be the best way to receive orders from the President of the United States? If he gave an order to go to a country and present his plan for global economic change, what would it take to follow the order? Would you feel comfortable receiving that assignment from a friend? Would a call from an agent be enough? Or would you prefer to get this type of duty from him in person?

To answer the question some of you may be wondering, no, I have never heard the audible voice of God or been to the throne room. Some people want and crave to hear God's voice with their physical ears or be taken to the throne room. Be careful what you ask for. If He allows these experiences, it's not so you can brag about it, feel hyper-spiritual, or start to think you're more highly favored than others. It's to give you an assignment that He expects to be carried out. And the experience gives such intimate knowledge of God that no one would dare decline His order.

Below is an account of a throne room experience in scripture:

In the year that King Uzziah died, I saw the Lord sit-ting on a throne, high and lifted up, and the train of His robe filled the temple. Above it stood seraphim; each one had six wings: with two he covered his face, with two he covered his feet, and with two he flew. And one cried to another and said: "Holy, holy, holy is the Lord of hosts; the whole earth is full of His glory!" And the posts of the door were shaken by the voice of him who cried out, and the house was filled with smoke. So I said: "Woe is me, for I am undone! Because I am a man of unclean lips, and I dwell in the midst of a people of unclean lips; for my eyes have seen the King, the Lord of hosts." Then one of the seraphim flew to me, having in his hand a live coal which he had taken with the tongs from the altar. And he touched my mouth with it, and said: "Behold, this has touched your lips; your iniquity is taken away, and your sin purged." Also I heard the voice of the Lord, saying: "Whom shall I send, and who will go for Us?" Then I said, "Here am I! Send me" (Isaiah 6:1-8, NKJV).

The assignment? Isaiah was to prophecy against the people and the land of Israel. Not a fun task. It reminds me of some of the prophecies and warnings the Lord has brought through John Paul Jackson. Everything was going great in our country when this servant started getting words of wisdom and revelation of what the Lord was going to do. Many did not like what was being said and did not want to receive it. Yet, here we are, seeing it all play out just as the Lord had told him.

Isaiah saw the Lord seated on the throne. He saw the temple and the seraphim. His lips were cleaned and the sin purged from him by a burning coal. If we suddenly find ourselves in a room difficult to describe, where acute awareness of sin occurs, there are angelic beings present, and the

The God Zone

Lord is sitting on a throne, a throne room experience is happening. This supernatural event is to drive one to accept the assignment the Lord wants and expects accomplished.

Revelation 4 gives another account of a throne room experience. John was taken in the Spirit to the throne room of heaven, where he saw God sitting on the throne. Angelic beings were there, and he had to use similes to describe the room. His assignment was to write down all the visions he saw regarding the end of the world and the dawn of the new earth and Jerusalem. In addition, he wrote seven letters to seven different churches, giving them a word from Jesus. The letters outlined each church's successes and failures.

The people who'd had a throne room experience were seers (prophets of the Lord) who were called to speak to a nation or the world at large. When God calls men to great and scary tasks, He will speak to them in a way that brings validity to the assignment. If God wanted me to go to a place where I was wanted for murder, asked me to present a demand to the president or king of that land with only a rod and a friend to go with me, a dream or vision wouldn't cut it. I would need something with more weight, something more substantial, something more tangible.

No matter what God wants us to do or tell, He will use whatever is necessary to make sure we hear Him and follow through with His command. Isaiah was a believer but was not walking with the Lord when He was taken to the throne room. He states that he and the people were unclean. During King Uzziah's reign, the Lord was not top priority. The king was doing what was right in the sight of the Lord, but the people were not.

Chasing Fire

At any time, whether we are walking with the Lord and obeying his commandments or not, He can choose to bring us to His throne room or speak to us audibly. There are no prerequisites. No man can dictate or decide how God will speak to another person. It is all up to Him.

Fourteen

Recognizing and Listening

"You are dead! I am going to kill you!"

A death sentence had been delivered by the angry, dark spirit that moved around my room like a dancing ribbon with hydraulics. Tears ran down my face as this entity spoke into my mind and pierced my spirit. Remembering the light beings from my youth, I found strength to pray a common, one-word prayer: "Help."

No answer. Though my eyes produced tears of worried hope, every once in a while, I looked up to the ceiling for the army of lights to show up.

Swiftly and powerfully, my bedroom door opened. I turned to face my roommate, Gina, and a woman I did not know. With determination in her stance and authority in her voice, Gina asked, "Is the devil in here?"

Through sobs I replied, "He is going to kill me."

"Oh no, he's not! He's a liar!"

She gave a speedy introduction of the woman with her.

Chasing Fire

While this woman was driving past our apartment, the Lord told her to stop because someone was under attack. After the introduction, these two women began to pray with fervency, confidence, and power. They commanded the dark spirit to leave in the name of Jesus. It obeyed.

Immediately following its departure, they laid hands on me and began to pray and prophecy over me the plans of the Lord, naming the places I would go and the things I would do for the glory of God. Peace was restored to me, and I learned more lessons:

1. There is another voice, and it is not God, but the evil one, the devil, Satan.
2. Like my sisters in Christ, I have power over him.

Anyone reading this testimony of the attack I experienced can recognize that whatever was speaking to me was not the Lord. The spirit in my room was blatantly and clearly the enemy. Even with this knowledge, I began to believe two lies: 1. God did not love me, and 2. This thing was going to kill me.

The Bible teaches that Satan is the father of lies, the great deceiver who enjoys masquerading as an angel of light (John 8:44; 2 Corinthians 11:14.) Therefore, there are times we can be fooled. So it is imperative to learn to recognize the difference between God's voice, the devil's voice, and our own.

Recognizing and Listening

Characteristics of God's Voice

1. No matter what He says, it will be wrapped in love.

I am so thankful for my earthly father. Praise God! I believe He used my dad to give me examples of how the perfect Father communicates and wants to relate to each of us. My dad showed great love toward me and my sisters when speaking to us. This love was evident even when we were in trouble and about to experience consequences for our actions. My tears were never a result of the consequence but a result of the fact that I had disappointed him. I was convicted but never condemned. As I entered my teen years, I learned to trust my dad with my mistakes. Whenever I did something that was totally unwise and against his teachings, I came to him, crying and confessing what had happened. He always forgave me and would give me either wisdom for handling the situation next time or a consequence or both.

God's method of communicating may be firm and stern but never mean or mocking. It may bring conviction but not condemnation. God will show ridiculous love toward us, even when correction is involved. There is no condemnation with Him. A direction will be wrapped in love. God will reveal the way and then leave us the power to trust and follow Him in that direction. But we don't have to follow. God gave this free will to Adam and Eve in the beginning. He told them not to eat of the fruit from the tree of the knowledge of good and evil. God asks us to stay clear of some modern-day trees due to the significant consequences. Smoking has the potential of killing and shortening your

Chasing Fire

life. Drug and alcohol abuse runs the potential of taking you out and others as well. Everything the Lord directs us to do or not do is linked to His genuine love and care for us. He wants His best for all of us.

Beloved, let us love one another, for love is of God; and everyone who loves is born of God and knows God. He who does not love does not know God, for God is love (1 John 4:7-8, NKJV).

There is therefore now no condemnation to those who are in Christ Jesus, who do not walk according to the flesh, but according to the Spirit (Romans 8:1, NKJV).

And the Lord God commanded the man, saying, "Of every tree of the garden you may freely eat; but of the tree of the knowledge of good and evil you shall not eat, for in the day that you eat of it you shall surely die" (Genesis 2:16-17, NKJV).

2. He will never contradict His Word (the Bible).

The Bible is the standard to test the spirits. If any voice or person delivers a message "from God," and it does not reflect God's characteristics and attributes and does not match the Word of God, the message is from a deceiver or someone in deception.

For example, I had a so-called prophet tell me that I was not a blessing to my church and had caused great pain

Recognizing and Listening

to the members because I did not choose the songs he wanted to use in the worship service. I also had a so-called prophet give me a word that immediately started to build pride and puff me up. Both of these were from a false spirit and not the Lord. God's Word teaches that all words should bring glory to Him, not to a person. The Word also teaches that humility is a character trait we should keep and build. Pride is not.

Beloved, do not believe every spirit, but test the spirits, whether they are of God; because many false prophets have gone out into the world (1 John 4:1, NKJV).

When pride comes, then comes shame; but with the humble is wisdom (Proverbs 11:2, NKJV).

Pride goes before destruction, and a haughty spirit before a fall (Proverbs 16:18, NKJV).

Therefore, whether you eat or drink, or whatever you do, do all to the glory of God (1 Corinthians 10:31, NKJV).

Read and study the Bible. It teaches us how to discern what is of God and what is not. If we imprint the scriptures on our hearts and minds, we'll quickly recognize what is false and what is true. The identity God has assigned to us is in the Word. Any message that contradicts who God says

157

Chasing Fire

we are is from a false spirit. Any message that contradicts who Jesus is comes from a false spirit. We must keep the Word of God before us. It is the litmus test for every message that comes our way.

> *Husbands, love your wives, just as Christ also loved the church and gave Himself for her, that He might sanctify and cleanse her with the washing of water by the word* (Ephesians 5:25-26, NKJV).

> *And be renewed in the spirit of your mind, and that you put on the new man which was created according to God, in true righteousness and true holiness* (Ephesians 4:23-24, NKJV).

3. His words will produce or increase the fruit of the Spirit in us.

Once the word is heard, it will agitate the flesh and cause the spirit to grow. For example, the Lord gave me a directive that is building humility and patience in my character. My spirit is at war with my desires to be independent of His provision and not let go of a career that was puffing me up. In addition, God is leading me to a new place, and I don't have all the details, which means I am forced to practice patience. This is very challenging. But glory to God, we are all more than conquerors. Greater is He in me than he who is in the world.

> *Now the works of the flesh are evident, which are: adultery, fornication, uncleanness, lewdness, idolatry, sor-*

Recognizing and Listening

cery, hatred, contentions, jealousies, outbursts of wrath, selfish ambitions, dissensions, heresies, envy, murders, drunkenness, revelries, and the like; of which I tell you beforehand, just as I also told you in time past, that those who practice such things will not inherit the kingdom of God. But the fruit of the Spirit is love, joy, peace, longsuffering, kindness, goodness, faithfulness, gentleness, self-control. Against such there is no law. And those who are Christ's have crucified the flesh with its passions and desires. If we live in the Spirit, let us also walk in the Spirit (Galatians 5:19-25, NKJV).

4. His words will cause a greater hunger for Him in us.

It's a supernatural thing. Hearing, recognizing, and receiving the voice of the Lord gives us a spiritual thirst and hunger to hear and experience Him again. Whether it is a message of hope, encouragement, correction, or just to bring knowledge that He is there, our need to hear from Him grows. The fruit of His words builds our faith and trust in Him, and we want more of Him.

Characteristics of Satan's Voice

1. No matter what he says, it will be wrapped in hate.
2. He will always twist and contradict God's word (the Bible).
3. His words will produce and increase the desires of the flesh.
4. His words are meant to cause a rift in our relationship with God, the Creator.

Chasing Fire

Notice how these four things are the direct opposite of the characteristics of God's voice. The enemy of our souls works through his dominion (demons, strongholds, powers, principalities, and rulers of darkness) and people. His goal is to take as many people to hell with him as possible. The next best thing is to steal, kill, and destroy anything God has for you, including your destiny. He, the created, got in a war with his maker, God. The end result was his demise. As he fell like lightening from heaven, he made a decision not to go down alone.

He does this through lying. He lies all the time. There is no truth in him. He began lying in the Garden of Eden, deceiving Eve by twisting what God said. He attempted the same thing with Jesus Christ. The devil used the scripture to try to get Jesus to usurp His calling and purpose. If he used the tactic with God incarnate, then of course he will use it on us. He's evil. So beware of his devices.

For we do not wrestle against flesh and blood, but against principalities, against powers, against the rulers of the darkness of this age, against spiritual hosts of wickedness in the heavenly places (Ephesians 6:12, NKJV).

Then the devil took Him up into the holy city, set Him on the pinnacle of the temple, and said to Him, "If You are the Son of God, throw Yourself down. For it is written: 'He shall give His angels charge over you,' and 'In their hands they shall bear you up, lest you dash your foot against a stone.'" Jesus said to him, "It is written

again, 'You shall not tempt the Lord your God'"
(Matthew 4:5-7, NKJV).

The thief does not come except to steal, and to kill, and to destroy. I have come that they may have life, and that they may have it more abundantly (John 10:10, NKJV).

Characteristics of Our Voice

1. It speaks to us in the first person.
2. It is the fruit of the mind of Christ or thoughts projected to us from the enemy or the world.

When we have a thought and the phrase starts with "I," then that thought or message is coming from within us. We have a brain and are able to make decisions, think, ponder, and meditate. Whatever comes after "I" will determine where the thought is derived from. Remember, what we allow in and receive as truth over time is what will come out of us. If the statement contradicts who God says you are, then it is a lie. If it is against promises God has outlined in His Word, then it is a lie. Find the scripture that refutes it and speak it out loud over yourself. Catching ourselves thinking is very hard. We have to work at it.

Once we determine where the voice is coming from, we have to decide whether or not to listen to it. If it is the Lord, stop and acknowledge that you hear Him. Talk back and see if there is anything else He wants to say. Listen. If it is the enemy, command the thought and him to leave im-

Chasing Fire

mediately. He is not worthy of being responded to in any other way.

If the voice is ours and does not reflect the mind of Christ, we need to take that thought captive and replace it with absolute truth. If the thought is a directive leading to action or behavior, the action or behavior should glorify God and agree with His statutes and expectations. It should not lead to harming ourselves or others in the short or long term.

For the weapons of our warfare are not carnal but mighty in God for pulling down strongholds, casting down arguments and every high thing that exalts itself against the knowledge of God, bringing every thought into captivity to the obedience of Christ (2 Corinthians 10:4-5, NKJV).

Recognizing and listening to what we hear in our minds takes focus. We must be deliberate in paying attention to the thoughts that play in our mind. The thought leads to an action, the accepted action becomes a habit, and the habit forms character. Our character needs to reflect the person and image of Christ. He is our example. He heard His Father in heaven and followed everything He said. Yes, Christ is God but He did it perfectly while under temptation as a man. With the help of the Holy Spirit and a determination to be diligent in living in a Christ-like way, we will be successful.

Deterrents to hearing God clearly are like radio static.

Recognizing and Listening

If you tune your eyes and ears to the things of God more than to the messages and things of the world, you will hear Him more clearly. For example, if we feed our minds with television or Internet images that deflate the need for purity or righteousness, then when the pure and righteous One comes, we tune Him out. We have trained our spirit not to listen but to ignore Him. But if we feed our minds with television or Internet images that increase our need to walk in purity and righteousness, then when the pure and righteous One comes, we're eager to hear Him. And we do.

Another static-like deterrent to hearing God is unresolved sin or choosing deliberately to transgress, understanding the decisions are compromising the truth. For example, believing you are to enter into a relationship with a married person is not truth. Spiritualizing it and trying to cover it with prayer and seeking out those who approve it creates static. Then someone comes with truth, explaining that it is not the Lord, but he is ignored, the Holy Spirit is ignored, and the Word of God is ignored. The conscience becomes seared and delivers us over to the action of the planted lie (Romans 1:28).

Physical noise, chaos, and busyness can function as static. If you need noise to help you fall asleep, put on a sermon or praise and worship music. Have times when there is no noise around you. Walk in peace and ask the Lord to keep chaos from you. Chaos, like busyness, bogs us down with weariness and physical fatigue. It's okay to have a full plate as long as it is what we are called to do. To know that, we must listen for the leading of God, the Holy Spirit. If your life is so crazy that you don't have time to spend

Chasing Fire

with the Father or His Word on a daily basis, something needs to come off the plate. God wants an intimate relationship with us. This requires spending more time with Him.

Building a relationship through conversation and spending time together brings intimacy. This is the kind of relationship we can have with God. God wants everyone to be saved, but He has given us the right to choose. Once we are in the fold and learn more of Him and His way through His Word, it becomes exciting to serve Him. Before you know it (like any other relationship that grows over time) he becomes your friend. Jesus is mine. Through Him, my Father in Heaven is a friend to me too!

Before I went public with this testimony, some knew my name, but very few knew of my experiences with God and hearing His voice. These experiences are precious pearls to me. To share them openly would mean risking more rejection (which you know is my Achilles heel) and giving people a reason to think I was crazy. But how selfish of me to hide what God wants revealed to the world! He loves everyone. He sent His Son, Jesus, to conquer sin and death for everyone. God speaks and He is passionate for everyone to hear.

Conclusion

While living in the East Bay Area and attending the Vineyard Church, I was fortunate to meet and hear the worship singing of JoAnn McFatter. An angelic voice came through her mouth as she sang for us one Sunday. Her talent for music and singing was clear, but an anointing rested on the tunes that permeated the atmosphere. This was strikingly alluring, but what was more interesting to me was that she sang what she meant. It was evident that the words were real to her. She was singing from her heart.

Magnificent Obsession, one of the songs she sang, captured my attention because it was a love song to Jesus like I had never heard before. She sang about how her passion for Him burns like fire.

I thought, how can you love Jesus like this? How can you love God with such pure passion? As I pondered her relationship with God, the Lord answered my question and simply said, "Follow Me."

I thought I already was, but I listened to Him and in my mind I said that I would. From that day to now, my life has been ridiculously wonderful. He has never failed me. He has kept me, guided me, healed me, and done many other things. Even in times of trouble or difficulty, my feet have not been moved and He has kept all His promises. Now God is my magnificent obsession, and I sing JoAnn's song sincerely.

This is for all of us. Being in relationship with God and hearing Him are meant to be the order of the day and not

Chasing Fire

just for a season. We are told in Genesis that Adam walked with God in the cool of the day. I often wonder what they spoke of. However, I have my own conversations with Him. We all should. God the all-consuming fire is chasing you. Chase back. Let Him be your obsession too. Give Him a chance if you have not already. Cry out to Him. I assure you, He will answer.

About the Author

Lisa Monique Martin was born in Southern California in a small beach community on a day she was supposed to die. A miracle baby was given to her parents, and they knew purpose was placed in their hands. At an early age Lisa received a call to serve God in foreign missions and teaching His Word through writing and speaking. This put her on a path for a love of God's Word, compassion for the lost, and a head on collision with the enemy.

After deep rebellion against all she had been taught, the Lord met her in a supernatural way, forgave her sins, healed her broken heart, and put her back on the path ordained for her to walk. This journey has given her a deep understanding of God and His Word and victory over the enemy. Her walk with Jesus and the Holy Spirit have afforded her an abundant life and increased the fire of God that burns in her to preach the gospel for salvation and teach the Word for discipleship. Her ministry, Deep Blue Ministries, focuses on prophetic evangelism and sound biblical teaching regarding the prophetic ministry, our identity in Christ, and intimacy with the Father.

Lisa is a sought after Bible teacher who travels to speak at women's conferences and retreats. She also is a certified teacher for Streams Ministries and teaches the *Art of Hearing God and Understanding Dreams and Visions* courses developed by John Paul Jackson. In addition, she serves as a women's Bible study teacher and alongside her husband as Singles Ministry Liaison at her home church. Lisa lives in Austin, Texas, with her husband, Ron, and stepson, Jacob.

Contact Information

To book Lisa for your next event or enroll in one of the Streams Ministries courses with her, visit her website at www.deepblueministries.com or email her at info@deepblueministries.com. To connect with her personally, friend her on Facebook or follow her on Twitter @LisaMonique7